Matthew Cooke

Insects, Injurious and Beneficial, Their Natural History and Classification

For the use of fruit growers, vine growers, farmers, gardeners and schools

Matthew Cooke

Insects, Injurious and Beneficial, Their Natural History and Classification
For the use of fruit growers, vine growers, farmers, gardeners and schools

ISBN/EAN: 9783337083380

Printed in Europe, USA, Canada, Australia, Japan

Cover: Foto ©Lupo / pixelio.de

More available books at **www.hansebooks.com**

INSECTS.

INJURIOUS AND BENEFICIAL,

THEIR

NATURAL HISTORY AND CLASSIFICATION

FOR THE USE OF

FRUIT GROWERS, VINE GROWERS, FARMERS,
GARDENERS AND SCHOOLS.

BY MATTHEW COOKE,

Late Chief Executive Horticultural Officer of California.

SACRAMENTO:
H. S. CROCKER & CO., PRINTERS AND STATIONERS.
1883.

Entered according to Act of Congress, in the year 1883,

BY MATTHEW COOKE,

In the Office of the Librarian of Congress, at Washington.

PREFACE.

This book is intended as an introduction to the study of Entomology. Up to the present time but little attention has been given to the study of the natural history of insects, especially by those who cultivate the soil; and the chief aim of this book is to introduce the subject in as plain language and as concise a form as possible, acquainting the student with the four states or stages of insect life, the transformations of insects, and the division or classification of insects into Orders and Families.

The plan of fully illustrating the work is adopted, thus introducing object-teaching to some extent, in order to aid the student in classifying the more common insects into Orders and Families.

As a rule which has but few exceptions, all the insects which belong to the same Family have similar habits; so that, by knowing to what Family any insect belongs, we know whether to regard it as an injurious or a beneficial insect, according to the habits of the other insects which belong to the same Family.

The information given as to their transformations is equally applicable to injurious, innoxious, and beneficial insects; but the illustrations chiefly represent those insects which are either injurious or beneficial, so as to give the student an idea of the appearance of members of the more prominent Families of insects which most interest the cultivators of the soil.

In the preparation of this book, I have kept in view the utility of such knowledge to the future husbandmen; and with the expectation that the study of Economic Entomology will, *from necessity*, be taught in the near future in the Public Schools, this book has been prepared with especial reference to being used as an introductory text-book, to prepare the student for the study of more advanced works.

To enable the teacher to teach this branch of natural history without previous preparations, a key to this book has been prepared and published in a separate volume.

The scientific, or technical names of the various insects referred to in this work are not usually given in the text, but will be found in the index, attached to the common names of these insects.

In the preparation of this book, I have freely consulted the works of Professors C. V. Riley, Cyrus Thomas, G. H. French and J. H. Comstock; also those of Doctors W. Le Baron, A. S. Packard, J. L. Leconte and H. A. Hagen; and I take great pleasure in acknowledging my indebtedness for the information I have received from their writings.

In the arrangements of the Orders I have followed that given by Dr. A. S. Packard, in his "Guide to the Study of Insects."

The Families of the Orders Lepidoptera, Orthoptera, and Nueroptera are given in full,* while only the most prominent Families of the other Orders are given.

Many of the illustrations are taken from my work, "Injurious Insects of the Orchard, Vineyard," etc.; others have been

---

* This refers only to those insects which are found in the United States of America.

added chiefly from Professor C. V. Riley; twelve were copied from Packard's "Guide to the Study of Insects;" several from the Smithsonian Institution publications, and also from Dr. Emmons' New York Reports; and Nos. 89 and 103 were copied from the Illinois Reports. The Pacific Rural Press kindly furnished the illustrations of scale insects and their parasites.

In preparing this book I have been ably assisted by D. W. Coquillett, Esq., late Assistant State Entomologist, of Illinois, in preparing manuscript, reading proofs, etc., which has placed me under great obligations to him.

M. C.

SACRAMENTO, CAL., November 1, 1883.

CONTENTS.

	PAGE.
Introduction	1
The Egg State	5
The Larva State	9
The Pupa State	15
The Transformations of Insects	17
The Imago State	23
The Internal Anatomy of Insects	34
The Seven Orders of Insects	36
Classification of Insects into Orders	36
Classification of Larvæ	48
Classification of Insects	50
Classification of Insects into Families	54
ORDER I. HYMENOPTERA, (*Bees, Wasps, etc.*)	54
ORDER II. LEPIDOPTERA, (*Butterflies and Moths*)	60
ORDER III. DIPTERA, (*Two-winged Flies*)	76
ORDER IV. COLEOPTERA, (*Beetles*)	80
ORDER V. HEMIPTERA. (*True Bugs*)	100, 105
SUB-ORDER I. HOMOPTERA, (*Similar-winged Bugs*)	100
SUB-ORDER II. HETEROPTERA, (*Dissimilar-winged Bugs*)	105
ORDER VI. ORTHOPTERA, (*Grasshoppers, Crickets etc.*)	108
ORDER VII. NEUROPTERA, (*Dragon Flies, May Flies, etc.*)	111
Scale Insects	114
Beneficial Insects	125
Collecting and Preserving Insects	130
Glossary	137
Index	147

NATURAL HISTORY OF INSECTS.

CHAPTER I.

Introduction.

Entomology is that part of Natural History which treats of insects. The term *insect* is derived from the latin word *insectum*, which signifies *cut into*, or notched, and it was applied to these animals on account of their notched or indented appearance (Fig. 1); they belong to the second division of the Animal Kingdom, called *Articulata*.

The vast Realm of Nature is divided into three Kingdoms, the Animal, the Vegetable, and the Mineral; to the first belong all animated beings, such as Beasts, Birds, Insects, etc.: to the second belong the various kinds of Plants, Mosses, Fungi, etc.; while the different Minerals, Rocks, the Air, Water, etc., belong to the third.

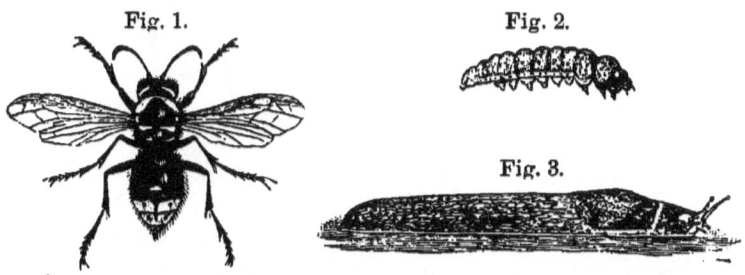

Fig. 1. Fig. 2. Fig. 3.

The Animal Kingdom is divided into four Sub-kingdoms, which are as follows:

I. BACKBONED ANIMALS (*Vertebrata*), such as Beasts, Birds, Reptiles and Fishes; these all have an internal skeleton, covered with flesh.

II. JOINTED ANIMALS (*Articulata*), such as Insects, Spiders, Crabs, etc.; in these the skeleton is external, and is divided into several rings, or segments, by transverse depressed circles.

These animals are readily distinguished by their jointed appearance, which is easily seen in the Caterpillar (Fig. 2) as it moves along.

III. SOFT-BODIED ANIMALS (*Mollusca*), such as Snails, Clams, Slugs (Fig. 3), etc.; these do not have the body divided into joints, nor are they furnished with either an internal or external skeleton, although they are sometimes inclosed in a hard covering or shell.

IV. STAR-FISHES (*Radiata*). These have the parts of the body radiating from the center, resembling somewhat an asterisk (*); they are found only in water.

Fig. 4.   Fig. 5.

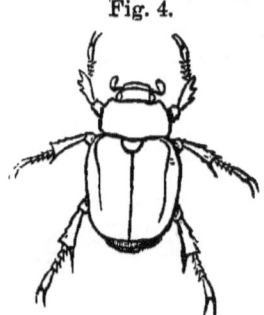 

Insects belong to the second division of the Animal Kingdom, called *Articulata*. This division, or Sub-kingdom, comprises five Classes, which differ from each other chiefly by the number of legs which they possess in the adult or perfect state. These five Classes are as follows:

I. TRUE INSECTS (*Insecta*), which are furnished with *six* legs, as the Goldsmith Beetle (Fig. 4).

II. SPIDERS, MITES, TICKS, etc. (*Arachnida*), are provided with *eight* legs, as the Red Spider (Fig. 5).

Fig. 6.   Fig. 7.

 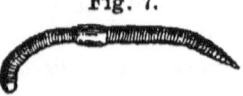

III. CRABS, LOBSTERS, etc. (*Crustacea*), have from *ten* to *fourteen* legs.

IV. CENTIPEDES, MILLIPEDES, etc. (*Myriapoda*), have *more than fourteen* legs, as the Julus (Fig. 6).

INTRODUCTION.

V. EARTHWORMS, etc. (*Annelida*), are entirely *destitute of legs*, as the Earthworm (Fig. 7).

The greater number of insects have the body divided into three distinct regions (Fig. 8), which have received the same names as the corresponding parts in the higher animals; thus, the first region, or part, is called the *head* (A); the second part, the *thorax* or chest (B); and the hindermost division is termed the *abdomen* or hind body (C).

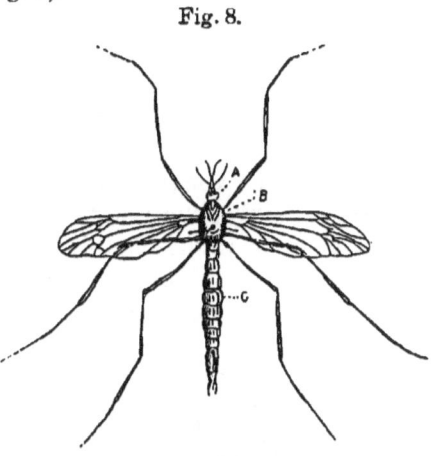

Fig. 8.

It is among the true insects alone that winged individuals occur, although all insects are not provided with these organs.

The Spiders (*Arachnida*) usually have the body divided into two distinct regions (Fig. 9), the head and thorax being merged

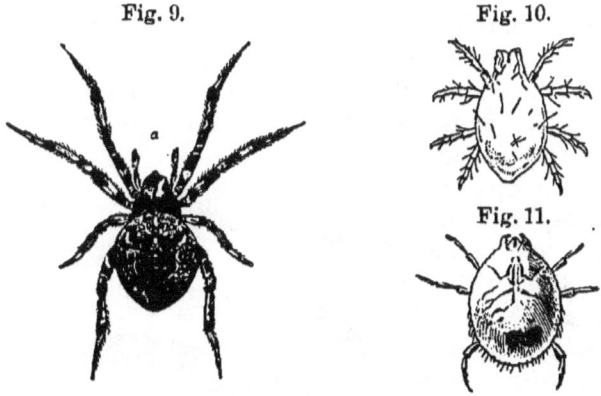

Fig. 9. Fig. 10. Fig. 11.

into one part; the thorax and abdomen are usually connected by a slender stem, or petiole. They do not pass through any changes or metamorphoses before reaching the adult state. So far as at present known, all spiders are predaceous, feeding upon insects, etc.; and one South American species, of very large size, is said to catch small birds by creeping up and springing upon them, like a cat.

The Mites and Ticks differ from the Spiders in having the three parts of the body closely united, as the Yellow Mite (Fig. 10), there being no distinct line of separation between the thorax and the abdomen. The young mites are usually provided with six legs (Fig. 11). Some kinds feed upon the leaves, etc., of various plants; others feed upon the eggs of insects or upon young plant-lice, such as the Phylloxera Mite (Fig. 12); and still others live parasitically upon different kinds of animals, such as the Sheep-scab Mite (Fig. 13.)

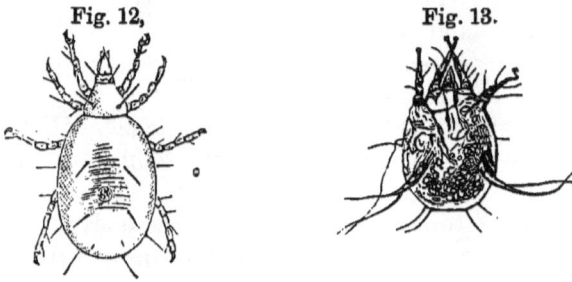

Fig. 12. Fig. 13.

The Scorpions belong to the same class as the Spiders, being provided with eight legs; their maxillary palpi (or feelers attached to the lower jaws), are frequently as long as their legs, and terminate in forceps-like claws. They are mostly predaceous in their habits.

The Centipedes, Millipedes, etc. (*Myriapoda*), are sometimes called "Thousand-legged Worms," from the great number of legs with which their bodies are provided (Fig. 14). They are readily divisible

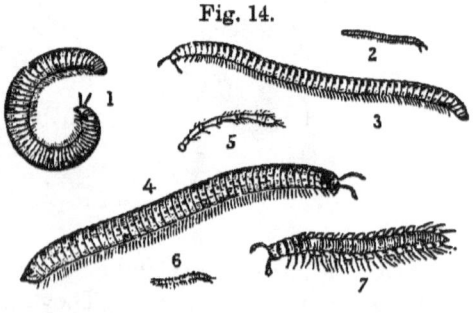

Fig. 14.

into two groups, according to the number of legs attached to each segment of their bodies. Some kinds have only a single pair of legs attached to each segment, while others have two pairs. By this character alone we are enabled to separate, at a glance, the injurious from the beneficial, since those which have only one pair of legs to each segment are predaceous, feeding upon Snails and other soft-bodied animals, whereas those having two pairs of legs to each segment. feed upon vegetable matter.

It will thus be seen that true insects belong to the first Class, which is known by the name of INSECTA. Having learned the position which these animals occupy in the vast Realm of Nature, a short account will be given in Chapters II, III, IV, and VI of the four states or stages through which insects pass, namely: First, the egg; second, the larva or caterpillar; third, the pupa, chrysalis or nymph; fourth, the perfect insect or imago.

Chapter V treats of their transformations (*metamorphoses.*)

CHAPTER II.

The Egg State.

The greater number of insects, such as Saw-flies (Fig. 15). Butterflies (Fig. 16), Moths (Fig. 17), Hessian Flies (Fig. 18),

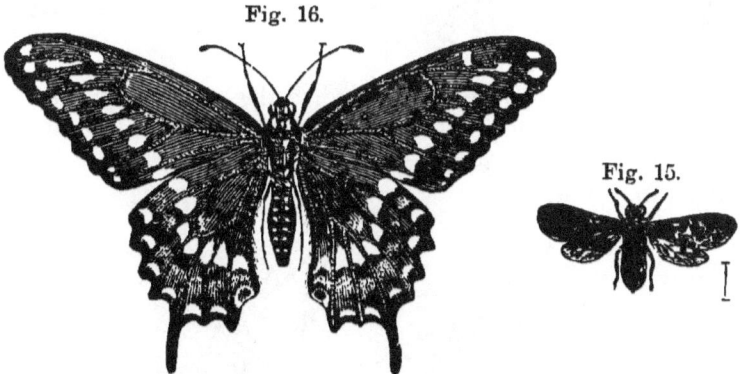

Fig. 16.

Fig. 15.

Beetles (Fig. 19), True Bugs (Fig. 20), Tree Crickets (Fig. 21), and Lace-winged Flies (Fig. 22), reproduce their kind by de-

Fig. 17.   Fig. 18.

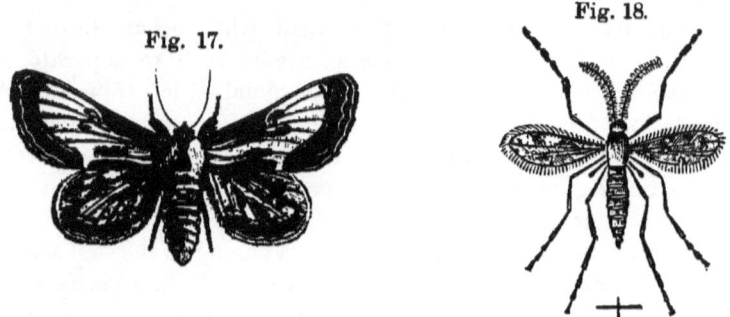

positing eggs, and are therefore termed "oviparous," (from the Latin *orum*, an egg, and *parere*, to produce).

Fig. 19.   Fig. 20.   Fig. 21.

Fig. 23,

Fig. 22.

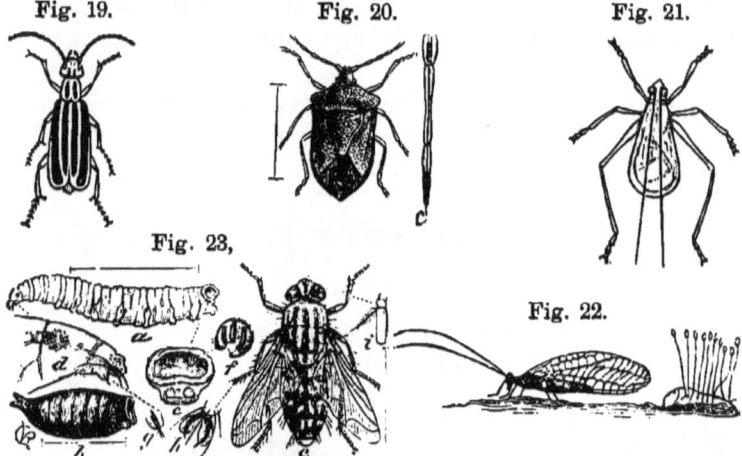

A few kinds of insects bring forth their young alive, such as the Flesh-fly (Fig. 23) and Plant-lice (Fig. 24), and are therefore called "viviparous," (from the Latin *vivus*, alive, and *parere*, to produce.)

Fig. 24.

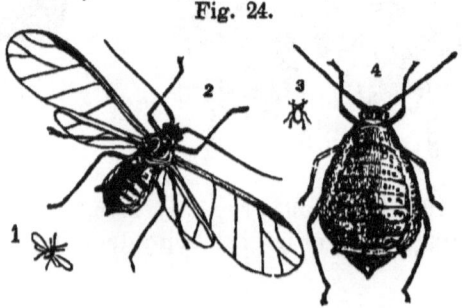

THE EGG STATE.

Fig. 25. Fig. 26.   Fig. 27.   Fig. 28.

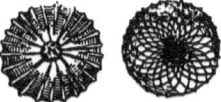

Fig. 29.

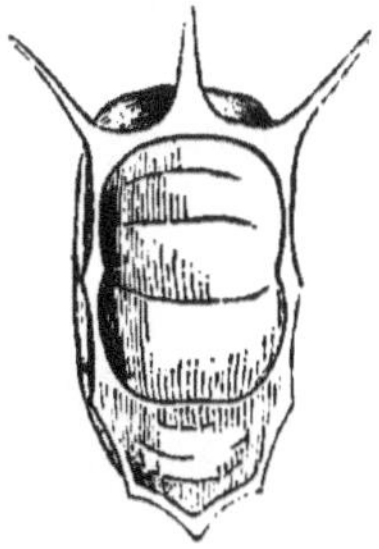

The eggs of insects are usually of a globular form, such as the eggs of some species of Butterflies (Figs. 25 and 26), but some are flattened, such as those of the Katydids (Fig. 27); while others are elongated, as those of the Tree Crickets (Fig. 28); still others, as those of the Tortoise Beetles (Fig. 29), are furnished with spines.

The surface of some insects' eggs are perfectly smooth (Fig. 27); others are ribbed (Fig. 25), and still others are covered with a net-work of raised lines (Fig. 26).

Insects deposit their eggs in a great variety of situations, but always where the caterpillar or *larva* as soon as hatched, will find an abundance of food within easy reach.

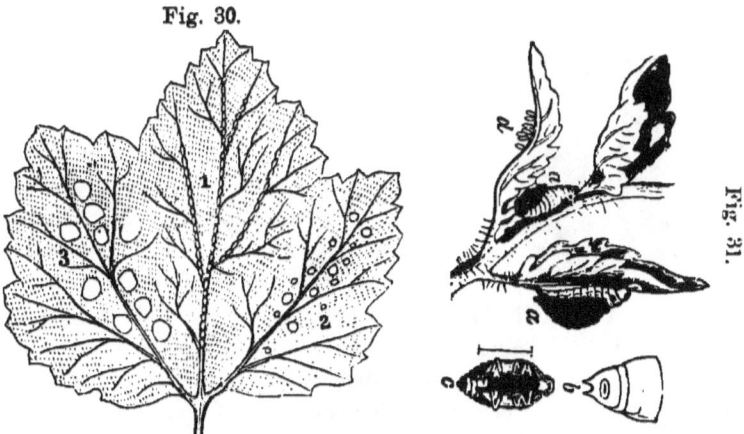

Fig. 30.

Fig. 31.

The greater number are fastened by a viscid liquid to the foliage of trees, plants, grasses, etc., as those of the Imported

Saw-fly (Fig. 30) and the Three-lined Potato Beetle (Fig. 31, *d*); while others are laid in rings around the branches or twigs of trees, such as those of DeLong's Moth (Fig. 32) and of the Orchard Tent Caterpillar (Fig. 33); other insects deposit

Fig. 32.   Fig. 33.

their eggs in punctures in branches, as the Gray Tree Cricket (Fig. 28), the Snowy Tree Cricket (Fig. 34), and the

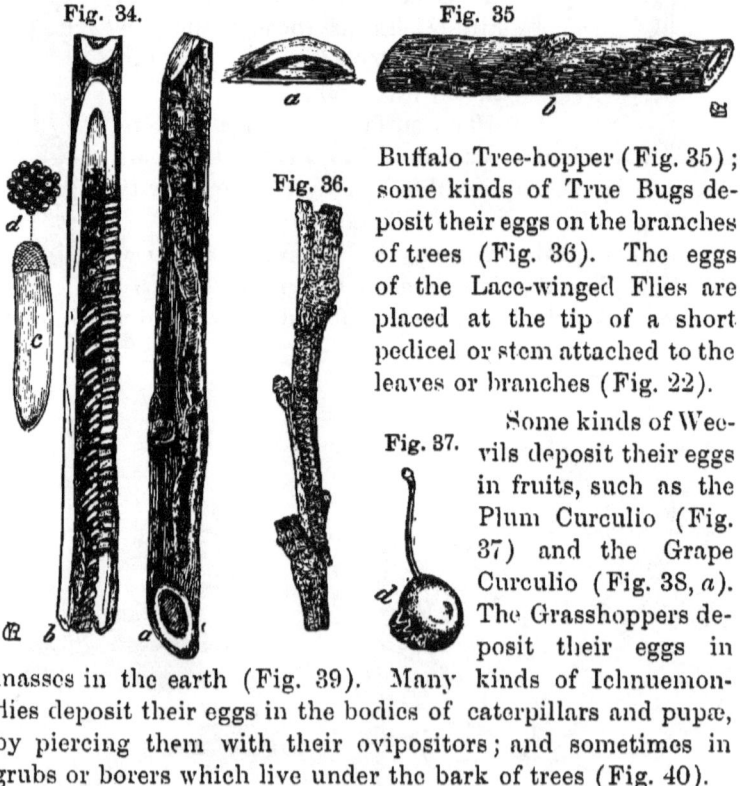

Buffalo Tree-hopper (Fig. 35); some kinds of True Bugs deposit their eggs on the branches of trees (Fig. 36). The eggs of the Lace-winged Flies are placed at the tip of a short pedicel or stem attached to the leaves or branches (Fig. 22).

Some kinds of Weevils deposit their eggs in fruits, such as the Plum Curculio (Fig. 37) and the Grape Curculio (Fig. 38, *a*). The Grasshoppers deposit their eggs in masses in the earth (Fig. 39). Many kinds of Ichnuemon-flies deposit their eggs in the bodies of caterpillars and pupæ, by piercing them with their ovipositors; and sometimes in grubs or borers which live under the bark of trees (Fig. 40).

The greater number of Gall-flies and Saw-flies make an incision in the leaves or twigs of trees, etc., in which they deposit their eggs.

Beetles of various kinds deposit their eggs in the ground; the Hessian flies, on the stalks of wheat; the Joint-worm flies, in the stalks of wheat, barley, etc.; the Army Worm moth, on the lower parts of grasses; the Butterflies, on the leaves of plants, etc., on which their larvæ are to feed; the Codlin Moth, on fruits; and the Borers, on the bark of trees and plants.

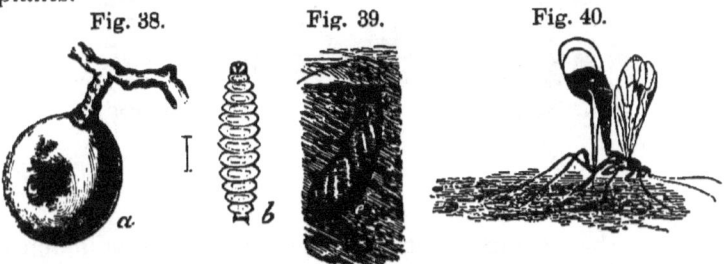

Fig. 38.   Fig. 39.   Fig. 40.

The egg of [an insect consists essentially of three parts, namely: the central germ cell, surrounded by the yolk and the outer shell.

The idea entertained by some persons, that many insects are produced spontaneously, is erroneous; all insects are brought forth by a parent, either as eggs or as living young.

CHAPTER III.

The Larva State.

Some insects, such as Grasshoppers, Earwigs (Fig. 41, *a*), Thrips (Fig. 42), and Soldier Bugs (Fig. 43, *b*), when they first

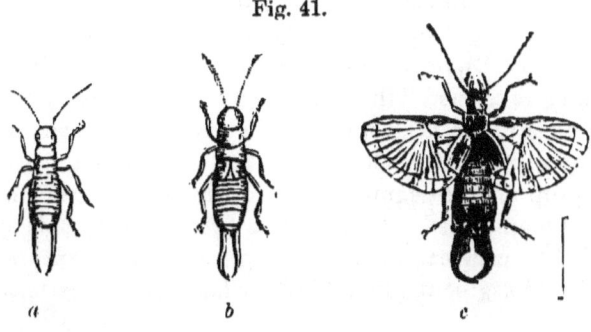

Fig. 41.

a   *b*   *c*

issue from the egg, very closely resemble the adult or parent insect, with the exception of being destitute of wings.

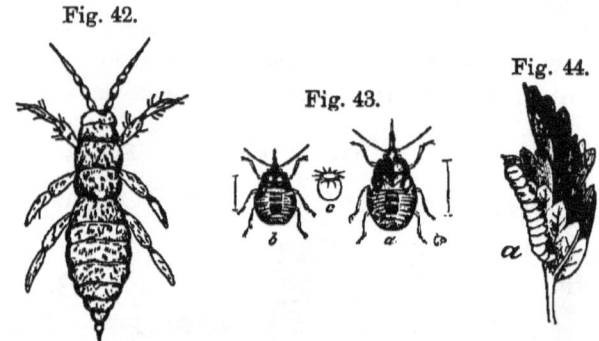

Fig. 42. Fig. 43. Fig. 44.

By far the greater number of insects, when first hatched from the egg, are worm-like, having the body elongated, and more or less cylindrical, and furnished with a distinct head (Fig. 48, A), armed with strong jaws, such as the Native Currant Worm (Fig. 44), the Army Worm (Fig. 45), the Wire Worm (Fig. 46), and the larva of the Lace-winged Fly (Fig. 47).

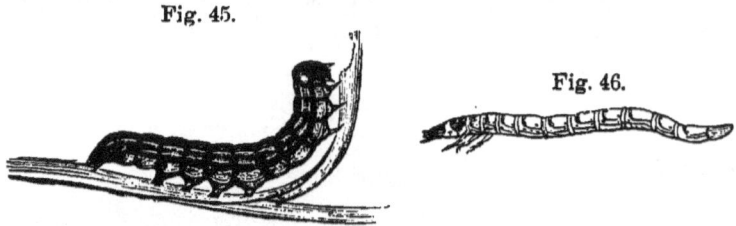

Fig. 45. Fig. 46.

The bodies of those larva which are worm-like are divided by transverse, impressed circles, into about twelve parts, called "rings" or "segments." The first three segments nearest the head (Fig. 48, B), represent the thorax of the perfect insect, and are therefore termed "thoracic" segments; the remaining nine segments (Fig. 48, C), represent the abdomen of the perfect insect, and are therefore designated the "abdominal" segments. On the top of the segment next to the head (or the first segment) is sometimes a horny plate (Fig. 48, G); this plate is named the "cervical shield;" a plate of similar texture on the last or anal segment (Fig. 48, F), when present, is termed the "anal plate." Sometimes there is a horn or spine on the top of the eleventh segment (Fig. 48, E); this is known as the "anal horn."

Fig. 47.

Fig. 48.

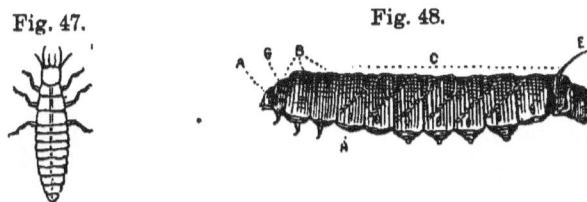

The greater number of larvæ have nine spiracles, or breathing pores (Fig. 48, H,) on each side of the body, one on each side of the first segment, and one on each side of the segments from four to eleven, inclusive.

When there is a line of any color extending along the spiracles, it is termed the *stigmatal line*. The back of a larva is termed the *dorsum*, and when there is a line in the middle, extending lengthwise with the body, it is termed the *dorsal line*.

A line midway between the dorsal and stigmatal lines is termed the *sub-dorsal line*. The under part of the body is termed the *venter*.

Some larvæ are perfectly smooth-skinned, as the caterpillar of the Turnus Butterfly (Fig. 49); others are more or less covered with tubercles, such as the caterpillar of the Cecropia Moth (Fig. 50); some are covered with warts, from which grow clusters of hair, as the caterpillar

Fig. 49.

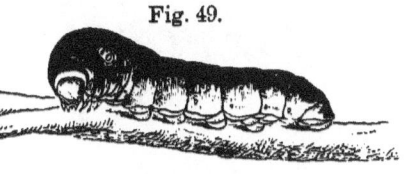

of the Tussock Moth (Fig. 51); still others are covered with small polished spots, termed *piliferous spots*, such as the Glassy Cut-worm (Fig. 52; see the enlarged segment), from each of which usually proceeds a fine hair.

Many kinds of larvæ are entirely destitute of legs; these are called grubs, maggots, etc.; for instance, the grub of the Plum Curculio (Fig. 53); of the Flat-headed Apple Tree Borer (Fig. 54); the grub of the Round-headed Apple Tree Borer (Fig. 55); and the larva of the Hessian Fly (Fig. 56.)

12   NATURAL HISTORY OF INSECTS.

Others are provided with six legs, as the grubs or larvæ of the Ground Beetles (Fig. 57).

Fig. 50.   Fig. 51.

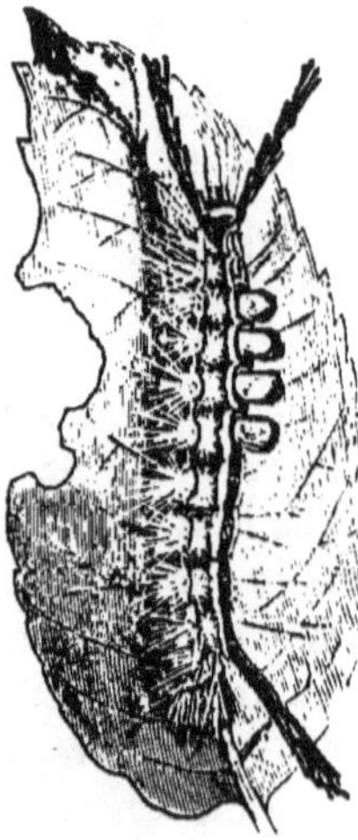

Fig. 52.

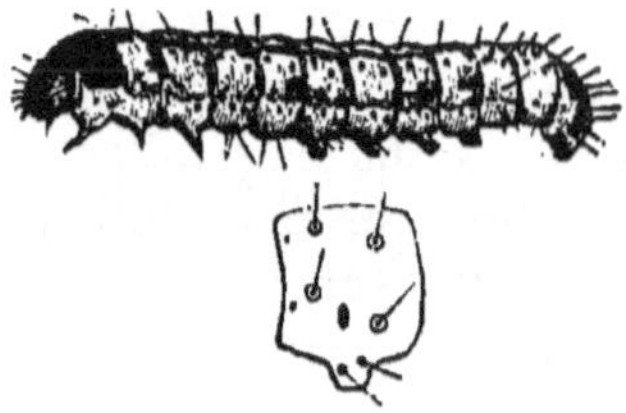

Larvæ having from ten to sixteen legs are called *true caterpillars*, such as the Span Worms (Fig. 58), which have only ten legs; the Glassy Cut-worm (Fig. 52), which is provided with sixteen legs. Caterpillars have a pair of horny legs

Fig. 53.   Fig. 54.   Fig. 55.   Fig. 56.

beneath each of the first three segments; these are the *true legs;* the additional legs are fleshy, and are usually encircled at the tips with a circle of minute hooks (Fig. 59); these fleshy legs are commonly called *pro-legs, prop-legs,* or *false-legs.*

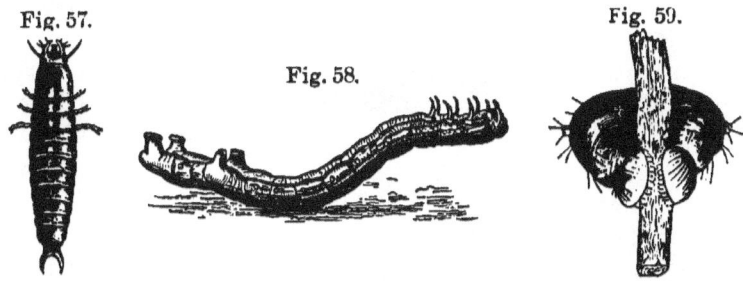

Fig. 57. Fig. 58. Fig. 59.

The greater number of larvæ which have more than the six thoracic legs, are furnished with ten pro-legs (Fig. 52); these are arranged in pairs beneath the sixth, seventh, eighth, ninth and twelfth segments; those under the twelfth segment are sometimes called the *anal pro-legs.* Larvæ having more than sixteen legs are called *false caterpillars,* such as the larva of the Imported Currant Saw-fly (Fig. 60), which is provided with twenty legs.

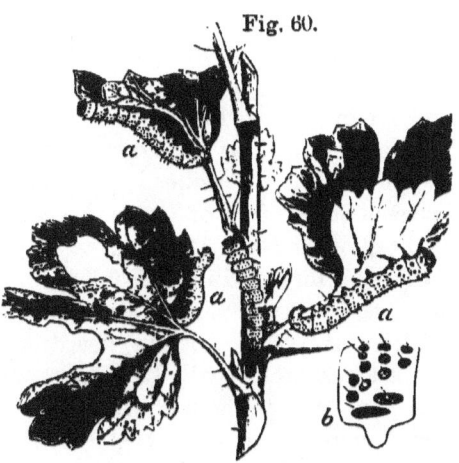

Fig. 60.

The pro-legs of these false caterpillars are not furnished with hooks at the tips.

The false caterpillars (Fig. 60), and also the true caterpillars, which are provided with sixteen legs (Fig. 52), in crawling about, move with a gentle undulating motion, while those which are provided with from ten to fourteen legs arch the body more or less upward. This is the most marked in the ten-legged caterpillars (Fig. 58), which are commonly called

"Span Worms," "Measuring Worms," or "Geometers." In crawling about they arch the body upwards (Fig. 61), by bringing their hind legs close to the front legs, then fastening itself by the intermediate and hind legs, it stretches out the body to

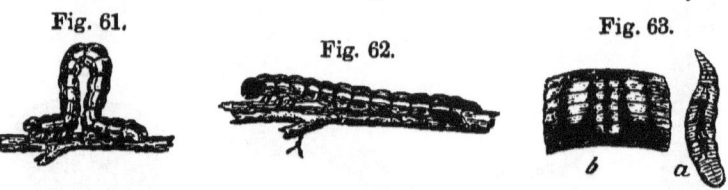

its full length (Fig. 62); the same movements are repeated in making the second and following steps.

The caterpillars that are provided with twelve or fourteen legs, in moving arch the body upward, in the same manner as those having ten legs, but to a less extent.

Some larvæ have the head soft and of no definite shape, such as the larva of the Syrphus Fly (Fig. 63); it is provided with a pair of hook-like jaws, which are usually curved downward. These organs appear to be unfit for masticating food, and are chiefly used to retain the larva in its place, or in holding its prey, and also to assist in moving around.

The soft, shapeless head occurs only in the larvæ of some kinds of Two-winged Flies, such as those of the House-fly (Fig. 64, A, represents the young larva, while at B is shown the same larva at a more advanced age).

These larvæ are always destitute of legs, and are commonly called "maggots."

It is usually in the larva state alone that the insect increases in size; the Butterfly or Bee, or any other winged insect, does not increase in size after its wings and other parts have acquired their proper shape and degree of firmness.

No larva, caterpillar, grub or maggot, is capable of producing eggs or bringing forth young,* these offices being performed by the adult insect only.

---

*Some writers claim that there are exceptions to this rule, but these exceptions are of very rare occurrence.

CHAPTER IV.

The Pupa State.

Those insects which, when they first issue from the eggs, closely

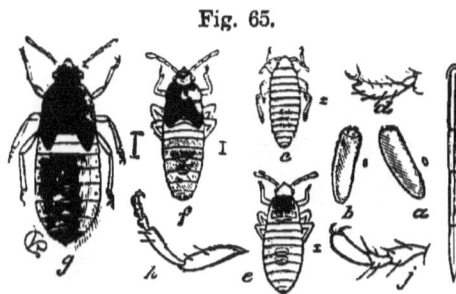

Fig. 65.

resemble the parent insect, such as the larva of the Chinch Bug (Fig. 65, c,) and the Harlequin Cabbage Bug (Fig. 66, a), do not differ very materially in form after they enter the pupa state (Figs. 65 g, and 66, b), except that they are provided with wing-pads, or cushion-like swellings in which the undeveloped wings are enveloped; they move about and take food as in the larva state.

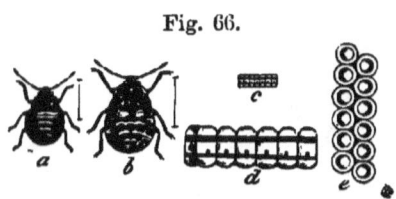

Fig. 66.

Fig. 67.

The pupa of those insects which were worm-like when they issued from the egg, are incapable of moving about and taking food, their legs and other appendages being folded up and encased in a sheath—such as the pupa of the Canker Worm (Fig. 67).

Fig. 68.

Fig. 69.

Fig. 70.

In some pupæ—such as those of the Beetles, Bees, Wasps, and many Two-winged Flies—the antennæ, wings and legs are enclosed in separate sheaths and folded on the breast, as the pupa of the Prionus Beetle (Fig. 68), the Flat-headed Apple-tree Borer (Fig. 69), and the Plum Curculio (Fig. 70).

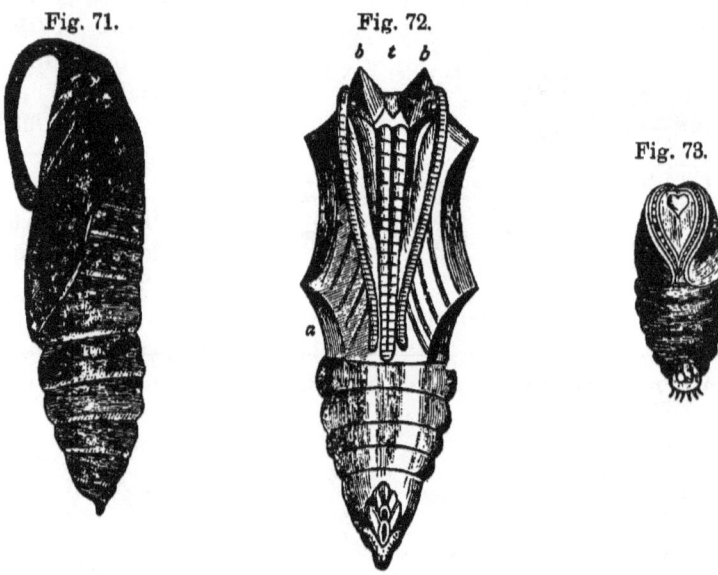

Fig. 71.　　Fig. 72.　　Fig. 73.

The pupa of Butterflies and Moths have the antennæ, wings and legs closely folded against the breast, and the whole is enclosed in a common covering or sheath, such as the pupa of the Tomato Worm (Fig. 71) and of many Butterflies (Fig. 72).

Fig. 74.

Fig. 75.

Fig. 76.

Pupæ vary in form; some have a smooth surface and are conical in form (Fig. 73); others are sometimes angulated, as the pupæ of many Butterflies, such as those represented in Figs. 74 and 75. The pupa of many kinds of Two-winged Flies are enclosed in the old larva-skin, which becomes contracted and hardened (Fig. 76). Pupa of this kind are said to be *coarctate* or covered, while the others mentioned above are said to be *obtected* or naked.

No insect can produce eggs or bring forth living young while in the pupa state; it is only in the perfect or adult state that insects can reproduce their kind.

CHAPTER V.

The Transformations of Insects.

Insects, with but few exceptions, pass through the four stages corresponding to the *egg*, the *larva*, the *pupa*, and the *imago*.

These different stages are easily observed in the life of the Archippus Butterfly. From the egg (Fig. 77, *c*, natural size; *a*, magnified), is hatched a small worm-like creature, which at

Fig. 77.

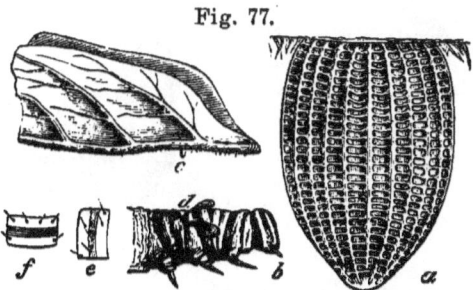

once begins to feed upon the leaves of the plant upon which the egg had been deposited by the parent butterfly; after increasing somewhat in size it casts off its old skin, and appears in a new and more commodious one. This process is termed "moulting."

When the time for casting its skin arrives, the caterpillar first spins a layer of silk upon some object, and then crawls upon it and fastens the hooks at the tips of its legs into the silk; it now remains quiet for a short time, when the skin on its back soon splits open, and the included caterpillar then crawls out. This operation is repeated at intervals three or four times, until the caterpillar reaches its full size (Fig. 78);

Fig. 78.

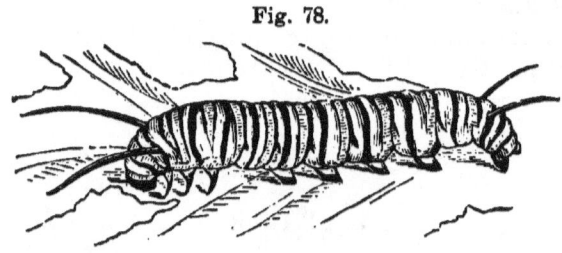

it then spins a bunch of silk to the under side of some object, and in this it entangles the hooks at the tips of its hind legs; then letting go its hold it hangs suspended, with the head and fore part of the body drawn slightly upward, giving to the body somewhat the form of the letter J (Fig. 79, *a*). In a short

Fig. 79.

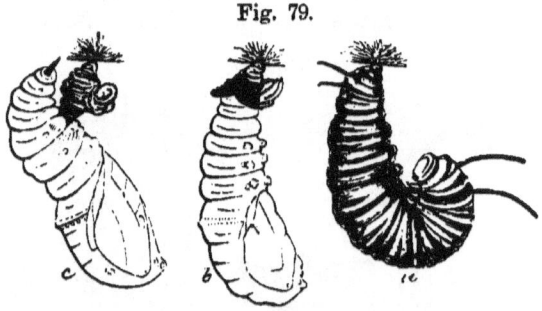

time the skin on its back splits open, and the included object, by elongating its body, pushes the fore part of the latter through the rent in the skin; the body is then contracted, or shortened, thus drawing the old skin backward; and this operation is repeated until the skin is worked back to and covers only the last two or three segments (Fig. 79, *b*). The pupa is attached, near the hind end of its body, to the old skin by a strong ligament. It soon withdraws the hind part of its body out of the old skin, and remains suspended by this ligament (Fig. 79, c); it then elongates its body and fastens the hooks at the hind end of the latter into the bunch of silk above the point where the old skin is attached, and by whirling around it breaks the ligament and dislodges the old skin, after which it remains perfectly quiet and gradually becomes contracted to its proper size and form (Fig. 80).

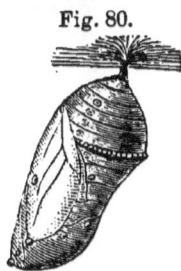

Fig. 80.

In the course of a week or so its colors darken, and the spots on the inclosed butterfly's wings can be quite plainly seen through the thin and nearly transparent pupa-skin; soon the latter is burst near the anterior or lower end, and the included butterfly comes forth. At first its wings are short and limp, but they gradually expand and harden, and soon attain their proper form and size (Fig. 81).

All insects which are worm-like when they issue from the egg, pass through the same stages as the Butterfly, although not always in the same manner. Some spin a shroud or cocoon (Fig. 82) around their bodies before entering the pupa state; others enter the earth and form smooth cells (Fig. 83);

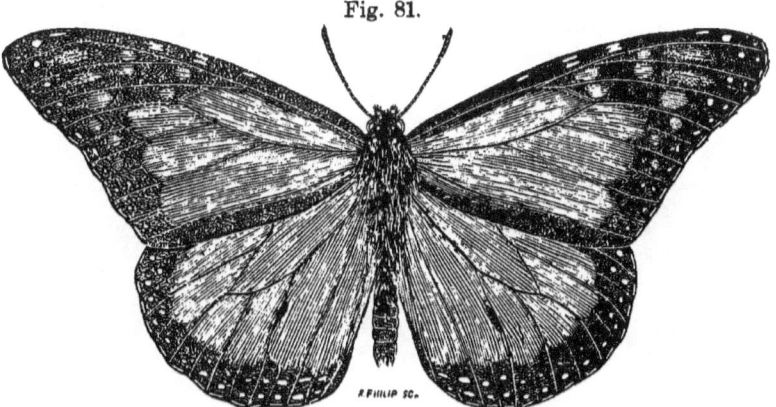

Fig. 81.

while still others assume this form in the plants or other substances in which they dwell (Fig. 84, b). Some suspend themselves by the hind feet alone (Fig. 79); others pass a loop of silken threads around the fore part of the body (Fig. 87, *b*). A few of the former merely work the old skin back upon the hind part of the body, where they allow it to remain, while in

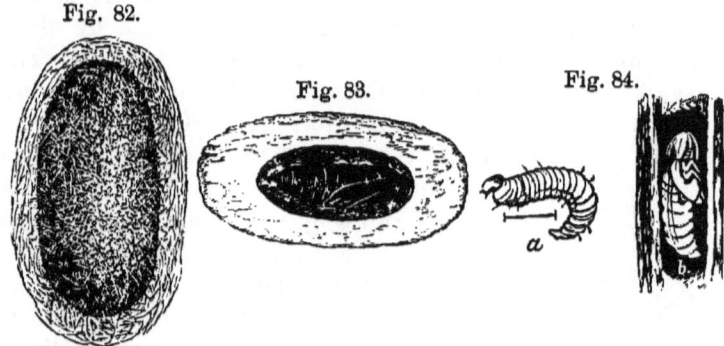

Fig. 82. Fig. 83. Fig. 84.

a very few the old skin is merely rent on the back, and nearly incloses the pupa. In the larvæ of a great many kinds of Two-winged Flies the larval-skin merely contracts and hardens (Fig. 76), completely inclosing the pupa.

Those insects which pass through the various stages detailed above, are said to have a *complete* transformation (metamorphosis).

But there are many insects (such as Grasshoppers, Plant-bugs, etc.), which, when hatched from the egg, very closely

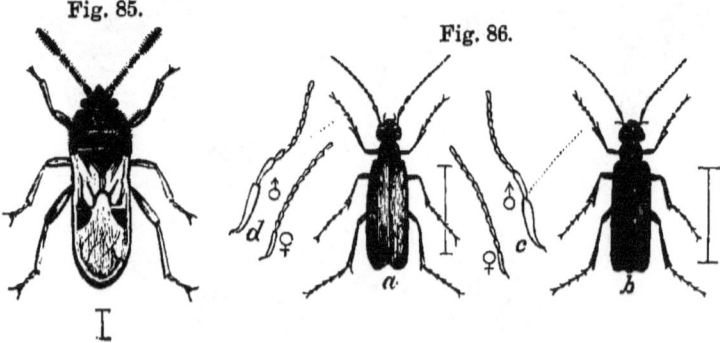

Fig. 85. Fig. 86.

resemble the adult or parent insect, except that they are always destitute of wings (Fig. 65, *c*); after increasing somewhat in size they cast their skins and appear in the same form as before, except that there is usually a pair of small wing-pads where the wings are to be in the perfect insect. At each succeeding moult, or casting of the skin, the form still remains as before, except that the wing-pads are larger (Fig. 65, *g*), and finally the insect moults for the last time, and appears with fully developed wings (as the Chinch Bug, Fig. 85). All this time it has been able to move about and to take food.

When about to cast its skin, the insect firmly fastens the hooks at the ends of its feet into some object; in a short time the skin on its back splits open and the included insect makes its escape.

Insects which pass through their different stages in this manner, are said to have an *incomplete* transformation (metamorphosis). Some insects which are worm-like when they issue from the egg, are active to a certain degree while in the pupa state; thus the pupa of the Lace-winged Fly, a short time before its final change, issues from its cocoon and fastens itself by the feet to some neighboring object; in a short time the skin on its back is rent, and the perfect insect makes its escape.

Fig. 87.

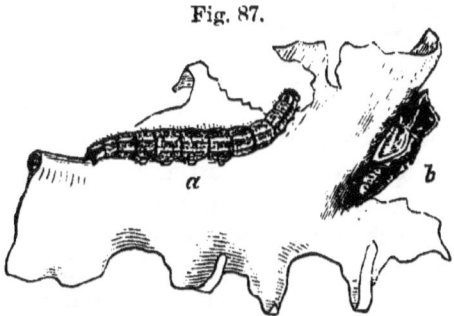

Some insects after issuing from the pupa are still enveloped in a thin film-like skin; this stage is usually called the *sub-imago*, and occurs among May Flies, and allied insects. They usually fly to the nearest plant, or other object, and soon cast off the film-like skin.

A few insects, like the Blister-beetles (Fig. 86), appear to pass through more than four stages. At the approach of winter the larva casts its skin and appears in a different form, commonly called the *semi-pupa*; it resembles the true pupa in being unable to move about and to take food, but differs from it in not having wing-cases, leg-cases, etc. In the following Spring it casts off its old skin, and again appears as a larva; the latter passes through the same changes as any other larva before reaching the perfect state.

The changes which insects pass through before reaching maturity have excited alike the interest and astonishment of mankind from the earliest ages. "To see the same animal appearing first as a worm-like creature (Fig. 87, *a*), slowly crawling along and devouring everything in its way, and then, after an intermediate period of death-like repose (Fig. 87, *b*), emerging from its quiescent state, furnished with wings adorned with brilliant colors (Fig. 88), and confined in its choice of food to the most delicate fluids of the vegetable kingdom, is a spectacle that must ever be regarded with the greatest interest; especially when we remember that these dissimilar creatures are all composed of the same elements, and that the organs of the adult were in a manner shadowed out in all its previous stages."

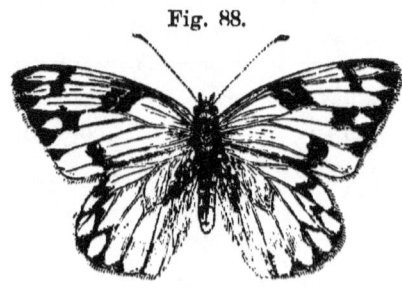

Fig. 88.

Let those who look with scorn upon the pursuit of Entomology as a study, learn that but few studies are better adapted to improving the mind and inculcating habits of observation and of accurate perception, while, as a whole, it has no small tendency to lift our thoughts to the great CREATIVE BEING—to Him who has designed the minutest part of the minutest object with reference to some particular use connected with the whole.

CHAPTER VI.

The Imago State.

By far the greater number of insects are provided with wings in the imago, or perfect state. Some, however, are destitute of these organs, and frequently very closely resemble the larvæ, or pupæ. This is especially true of some insects which are active during the pupa state, such as the Plant-lice, and some kinds of wingless Grasshoppers. The pupæ of the latter usually differ from the adults by having the wings twisted, so that the thin upper edge is nearest the under side of the body.

The body of the perfect insect (Fig. 86) is composed of three parts, the *head*, the *thorax*, and the *abdomen*.

THE HEAD AND ITS APPENDAGES.

The head is usually of a flattened, globular form. On each side is a large compound eye (Fig. 90), composed of a great many simple eyes placed close together. Besides the compound eyes, many insects have two or three simple eyes (*ocelli*), which are usually situated on the top of the head.* The antennæ *† or horns are two in number, and are usually placed below the eyes, but sometimes above them. The functions which these organs perform are not distinctly understood, but they are supposed to be connected with the sense of hearing; this supposition is strengthened by the fact that in some Lobsters and Crabs, a distinct organ of hearing has been found located at the base of the antennæ.

The antennæ of insects are composed of a certain number of joints which are numbered from the head outward; thus, the joint next the head is the first or basal joint, the last joint being the one at the tip or apex.

Some of the different forms of the antennæ are illustrated in the accompanying figures; the following are the principal kinds:

Filiform, or thread-like; of nearly equal width throughout its entire length (Figs. 91 and 94, *a*).

---

* See Fig. 89. † See Fig. 103.

24 NATURAL HISTORY OF INSECTS.

Clavate, or club-shaped; gradually enlarging toward the tip (Figs. 92 and 98).

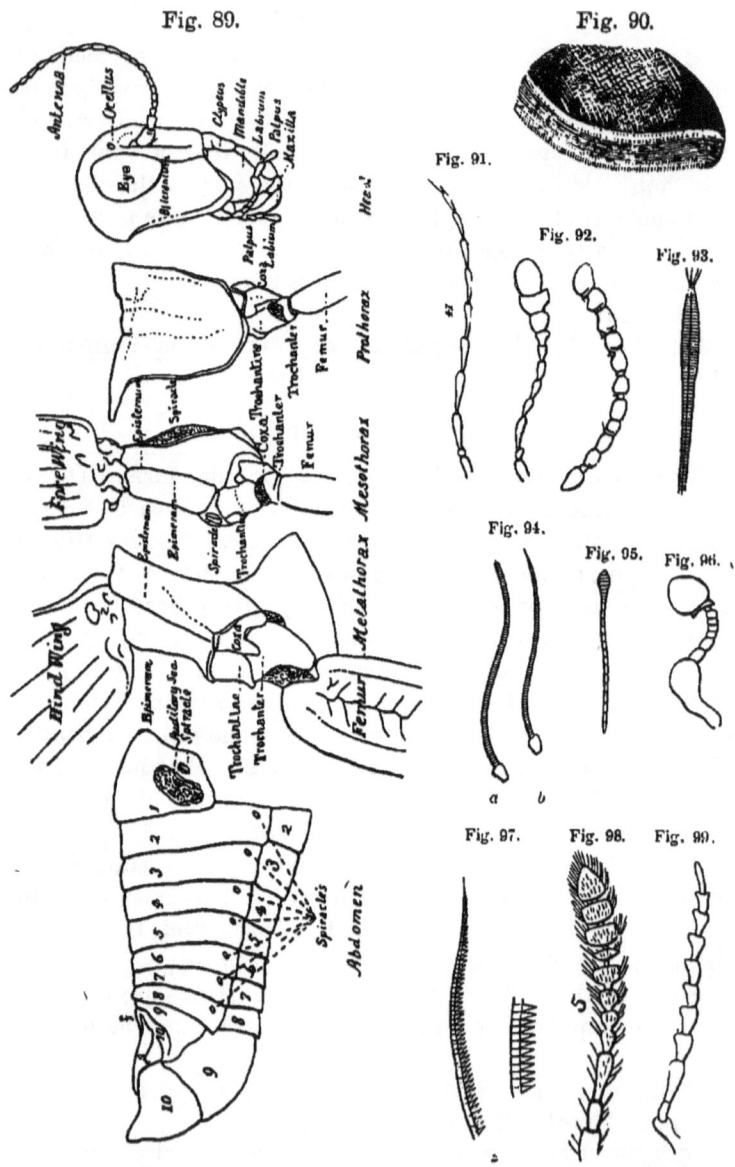

THE IMAGO STATE. 25

Fusiform, or spindle-shaped; largest in the middle (Fig. 93).
Setaceous, Setiform, or bristle-like; slender and tapering toward the tip (Fig. 94, *b*).

Fig. 103.

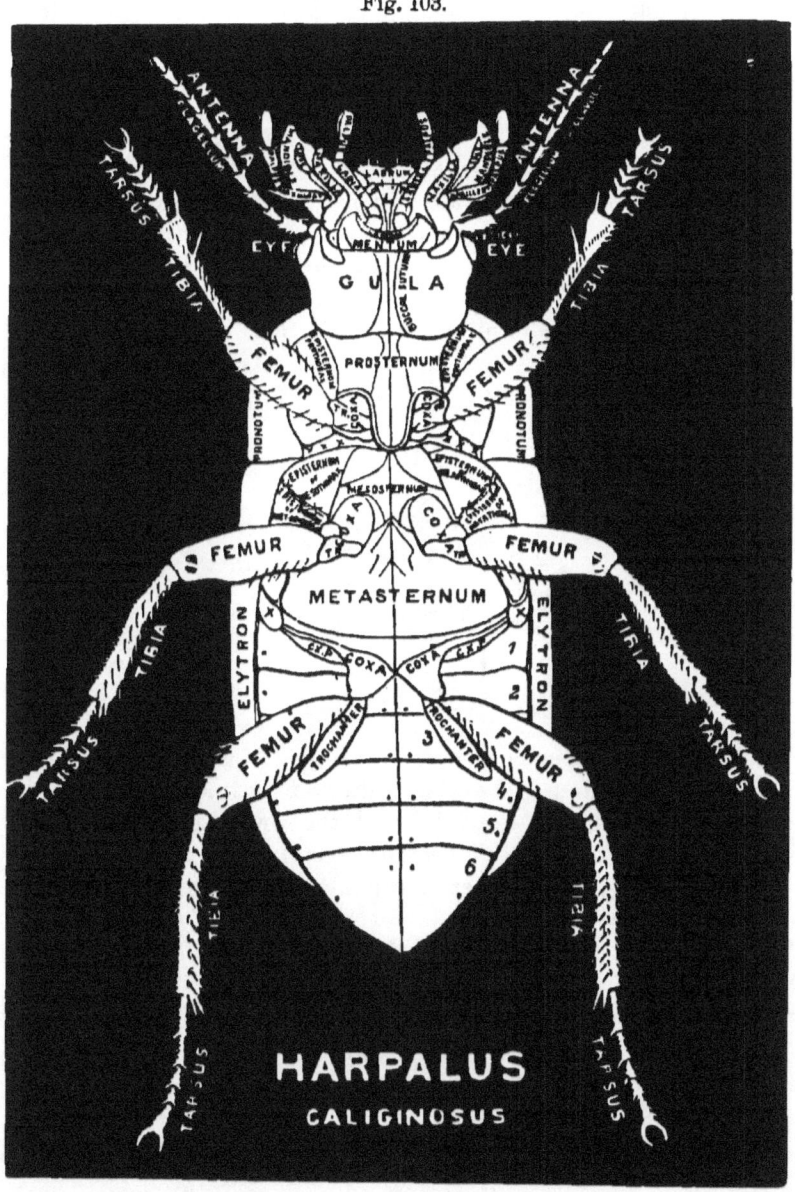

Moniliform, or bead-like; when the joints are more or less globular, resembling a string of beads.

Capitate, or knobbed; terminating in a knob at the tip (Figs. 95 and 96).

Serrate, or saw-toothed; when each joint is prolonged in the form of a small tooth, on the inner side at the apex or tip of each joint (Figs. 97 and 99).

Lamellate; when the terminal joints are prolonged internally in the form of flattened plates (Figs. 100 and 101).

Pectinate, or comb-toothed; when the inner angle of each joint is considerably prolonged at the apex (Fig. 102).

Bi-pectinate—Pectinate on both sides (Fig. 115, a., sometimes called *pectinate*).

[For other forms of antennæ, see Glossary.]

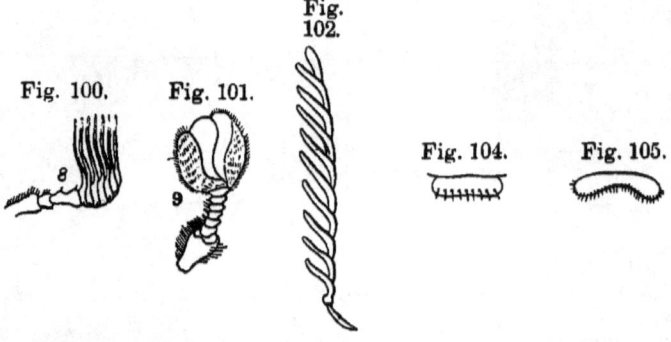

The mouth of such insects as masticate their food, consists essentially of four parts or sets of organs, namely: the upper lip (*labrum*, Figs. 104 and 105);*† the lower lip (*labium*, Fig. 106);*† the upper jaws (*mandibles*);*† and the lower jaws (*maxillæ*).*† These different organs are arranged as follows:

•
• •
• •
•

The upper and lower dots represent the upper and the lower lip, respectively; the two dots below the upper one represent the upper jaws, while the two dots below these represent the

---

* See Fig. 89. † See Fig. 103.

lower jaws. The upper lip is attached to the lower edge of the face, and aids in retaining the food in the mouth during the process of mastication.

Next to the upper lip is the upper jaws, which consist of two hard and more or less curved pieces (Figs. 107, 108, 109 and 110),*† which open and shut sidewise, instead of up and down, as the jaws of animals do; these are the true biting and masticating organs.

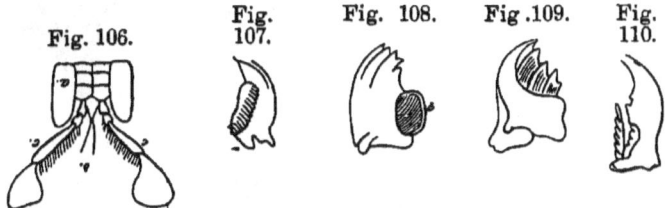

Fig. 106.   Fig. 107.   Fig. 108.   Fig. 109.   Fig. 110.

Next to these are the lower jaws, which are much softer than the upper ones; like them they open and shut sidewise, and their chief office seems to be to aid in retaining and masticating the food. Near the base of each lower jaw, on the outer side, is a jointed appendage, called the *maxillary palpus* (Figs. 111, 112 and 113).*† Below the lower jaws is placed the

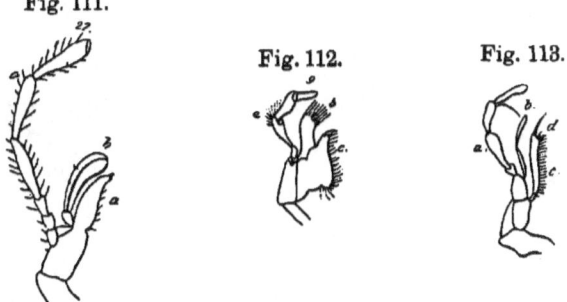

Fig. 111.   Fig. 112.   Fig. 113.

lower lip; this is used in retaining the food in the mouth; near the base are two jointed appendages, called the *labial palpi* (Fig. 106).*† When the lower lip is very narrow, the terminal portion is frequently called the tongue (*lingula*). It is attached to the upper and inner edge of the chin (*mentum*).†

---

* See Fig. 89.   † See Fig. 103.

There is sometimes a second pair of appendages attached to the lower lip, nearer its tip than the labial palpi; these are termed the *paraglossa*.

In those insects which obtain their nourishment by suction, such as Bugs, Butterflies, Moths, and the Two-winged Flies, some or all of the mouth parts are drawn out, or elongated, and several of them are sometimes united to form a single organ, or beak; in many insects—such as True Bugs (Fig. 114, *b*), Horseflies, etc.—the beak (Fig. 114, *a*,) is quite hard and fitted for piercing, while in others—such as the House-fly—it is quite soft and fitted for lapping. In the Butterflies and Moths it is usually quite long, frequently as long or longer than the entire body of the insect, and when not in use is coiled up like the hair-spring of a watch (Fig. 115, *g*), and concealed beneath the head.

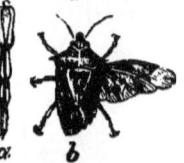

Fig. 114.

The posterior part of the head (or the part which is next to the thorax) is called the *occiput*. The top of the head (Fig. 116, *c*), is called the *vertex* or *crown*. Just above the upper

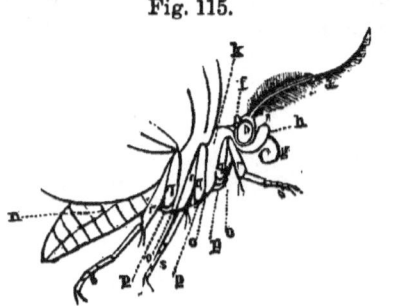

Fig. 115.

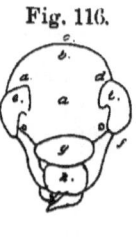

Fig. 116.

lip (*h*)* is usually a more or less square piece (*g*), divided from the neighboring parts by a suture or groove; this piece is termed the *clypeus*,* but in the Two-winged Flies it is called the *hyperstoma*. That part of the face which is between the clypeus and a line drawn from one antenna to the other, is called the *front*, while the part of the face which is between this and the vertex, is called the *forehead*. The cheeks are that

---

* See Fig. 89.

portion of the side of the head which is between the eyes and the mouth (Fig. 116, *f*).

THE THORAX AND ITS APPENDAGES.

Next to the head is the thorax, which is composed of three segments (Fig. 89). The first segment is called the *pro-thorax;* to this part is attached the first or anterior pair of legs;* the second segment of the thorax is called the *meso-thorax,** and to it are attached the middle pair of legs and the first or upper pair of wings when they are present; the third or last segment of the thorax is termed the *meta-thorax;** the last pair of legs are attached to this, and also the second or posterior pair of wings, when these members are present.

The upper part of the thorax is sometimes called the *notum*, while the under part has received the name of *sternum*. Each of these is divided into three parts, the same as the thorax; thus there is a *pro-notum* and a *pro-sternum*,† a *meta-notum* and a *meta-sternum*,† etc. The different parts of the legs are well illustrated in the accompanying figure (Fig. 117), where *e* represents the thigh, (*femur*) ; *f* the shank, (*tibia*) ; and *h* the foot, (*tarsus*); the latter is five-jointed, and the last joint is terminated by two claws (*i*). The part to which the thigh is attached at its upper end is called the *coxa*,*† and between them is sometimes a small piece called the *trochanter*.*†

Fig. 117.

The greater number of insects when in the perfect state, are provided with two pairs of wings.

In the Beetles the first pair are of a hard, bony texture, and meet in a straight line or suture on the back (Fig. 118); they are sometimes smooth, but are frequently covered with small humps (*rugose*), or with longitudinal ridges (*striæ*) (Fig. 119); they are nearly always covered with small impressed dots (*punctures*) (Fig. 120), as if pricked with the point of a pin; sometimes the outer edge of each wing is turned upward; this is called the *epipleura*. These wings are termed "wing-cases" (*elytra*) and are never used in flying.

---

* See Fig. 89. † See Fig. 103.

In Grasshoppers, Crickets and in some kinds of Bugs the anterior wings are more or less of a firm, leathery texture; in the Grasshoppers and kindred insects the front wings are sometimes called the *tegmina*, while in the True Bugs these organs have received the name of *hemelytra*.

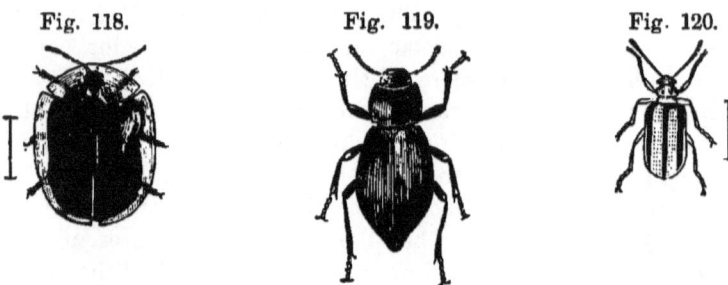

Fig. 118.   Fig. 119.   Fig. 120.

The Butterflies and the greater number of Moths have the wings (Figs. 121 and 122),* and also the body and its members,

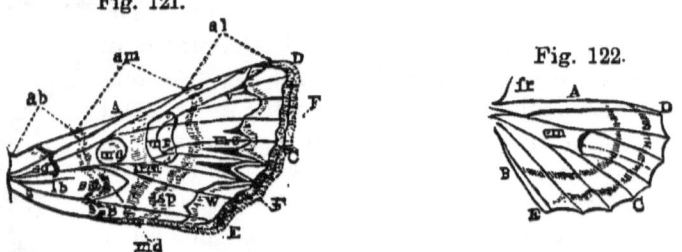

Fig. 121.   Fig. 122.

thickly covered with flattened scales of various designs; it is these which give the diversified colors to these insects. When these scales are rubbed off, the wings are found to be of a more or less membraneous texture (Fig. 123).†

In the Bees, Wasps (Fig. 1), Two-winged Flies (Fig. 124), Dragon-flies, Plant-lice and similar insects, all the wings are thin and membraneous; as are also the posterior wings in

---

*EXPLANATION OF FIG. 121.—*ab*, inner third of wing; *am*, middle third; *al*, outer third; *A*, costal edge; *B*, inner or posterior edge; *C*, outer edge; *D*, apex; *sd*, basal line; *sa*, transverse anterior line; *mo*, orbicular; *mr*, reniform; *um*, transverse shade; *sp*, transverse posterior line; *ms*, marginal line; *lb*, dentiform spot.

*EXPLANATION OF FIG. 122.—(Capitals same as in Fig. 121); *fr*, frenulum; *em*, lunule.

†EXPLANATION OF FIG. 123.— (Capitals same as in Fig. 121); *a*, antenna; *1*, prothorax; *m*, patagia; *k*, mesoscutum; *ab*, discal cell; *am*, discal cross-vein; above *al*, independent vein; *n*, abdomen.

those insects which have the anterior pair thickened (Fig. 114, b). The wings of the former kind are usually furnished with several veins (Fig. 125)* which are more or less con-

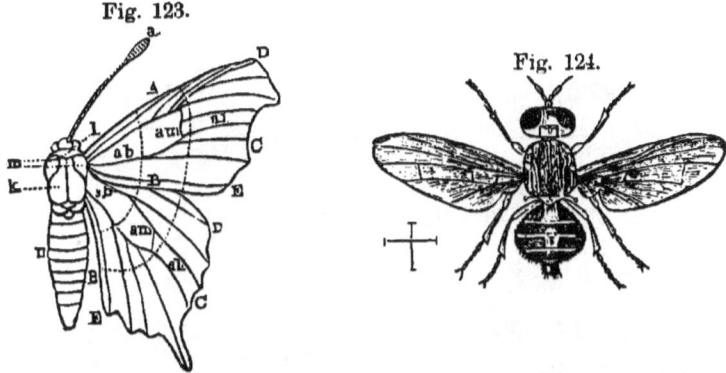

Fig. 123.

Fig. 124.

nected with each other by cross-veins or nervures. These veins and cross-veins form several enclosed spots, which may be likened to the panes of glass in a window; these are called cells. When one of these cells is entirely surrounded by veins and cross-veins, it is said to be *closed* (Fig. 125, 2, 2, 2); but if the outer or the posterior margin of the wing forms one of its sides, it is then said to be *open* (Fig. 125, 4, 4).

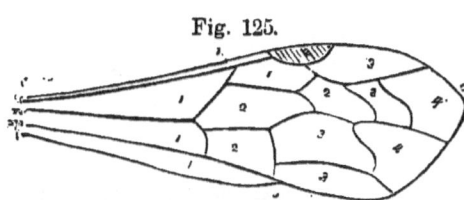

Fig. 125.

Naturalists determine the different genera and species of Plant-lice chiefly by the difference in the veining of the wings, these being the most reliable characters which these insects possess.

Fig. 126 † represents the venation of the wings of the Rose Aphis and Grain Aphis; Figure 127 represents those of the Apple-tree Aphis; and Figure 128, those of the Woolly Aphis.

---

* EXPLANATION OF FIG. 125.—*c*, costal vein; *sc*, sub-costal vein; *m*, median vein; *sm*, sub-median vein; *i*, internal vein; *1*, costal cell; *2*, (dark) stigma; *3*, marginal or radial cell; *1, 2, 3, 4*, (back of stigma and marginal cell) sub-marginal or cubital cells; *2, 3, 4*, (back of sub-marginal cells) discoidal cells; *2, 3*, inner and outer apical cells; *1, 1, 1*, (nearest the base) median, sub-median and internal cells; *e*, the apex.

† EXPLANATION OF FIG. 126.—1, basal cell; 2, first discoidal cell; 3, second discoidal cell; 4, infra-marginal cell; 5, first cubital cell; between 4 and 5, second cubital cell; 7, stigma; toward base of wing from stigma, costal cell; between 4 and 7, marginal cell. (The latter and No. 4 are sometimes called "apical cells.")

THE ABDOMEN AND ITS APPENDAGES.

The posterior division of the body of an insect is termed the abdomen, and contains the organs of nutrition and of

Fig. 126.

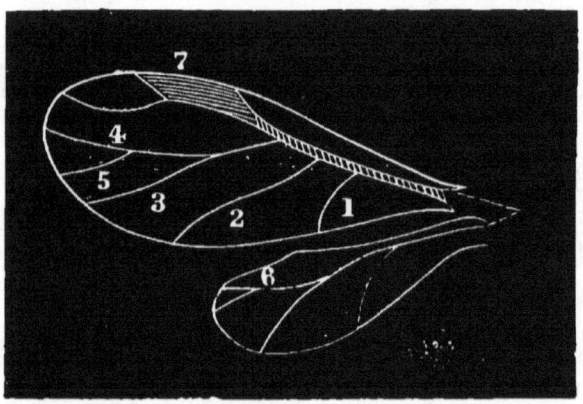

reproduction. It is sometimes united to the thorax by its entire width, but in some insects—such as Wasps, etc.—these two parts are connected by a slender stem, or petiole.

Fig. 127.   Fig. 128.

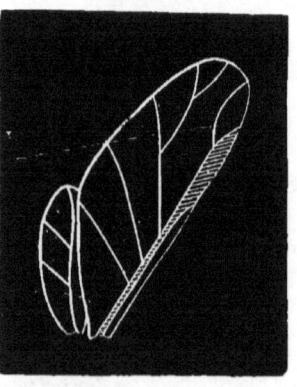 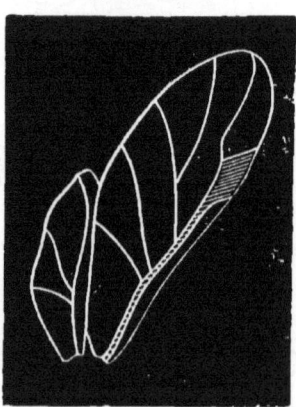

Along each side of the abdomen are the spiracles (Fig. 89), through which the insect breathes.

THE IMAGO STATE.

The tip of the abdomen is sometimes furnished with a sting—as in the Bees and Wasps—with which the insect defends itself. In other insects—such as the Saw-flies (Fig. 130)—it is furnished with a piercer or ovipositor (Fig. 129), which is

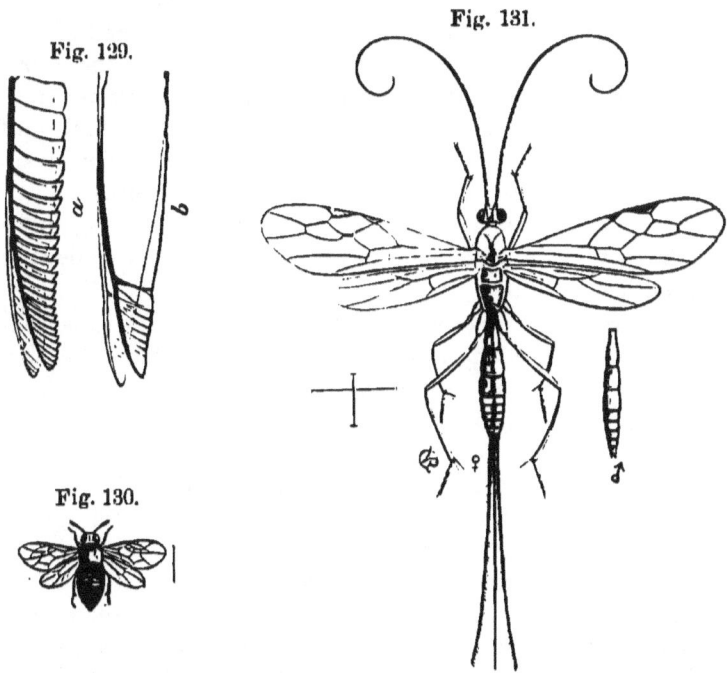

Fig. 129.

Fig. 130.

Fig. 131.

used for the purpose of making punctures in the leaves or twigs of plants, in which to deposit the eggs. The females of several species of Ichneumon Flies are furnished with an ovipositor, which is frequently as long as the entire body of the insect (Fig. 131), and composed of several thread-like pieces.

CHAPTER VII.

The Internal Anatomy of Insects.

The nervous system of insects consists essentially of two cords, extending the entire length of the body, and placed nearest to the lower side; these cords are situated one above the other, and the lower cord is enlarged at intervals into knots, called *ganglia;* from each of these knots a number of cords or filaments extend to the various organs. The fibers which compose these cords, separate at the anterior extremity of the body, so as to pass around the gullet (*œsophagus*), above which they again unite to form the brain, which is somewhat larger than the other ganglia.

The organs of nutrition consist of an alimentary canal, extending the entire length of the insect; it is enlarged in several places, and somewhat resembles the same organ in birds. The gullet (*œsophagus*) is terminated by a cavity resembling the crop in birds; next to this is a smaller muscular organ, analogous to the gizzard; this is followed by a larger and longer cavity, which is the true digestive stomach; this is contracted at the posterior end into the intestinal canal, which is enlarged at the posterior end into what is known as the *colon*. The liver and kidneys are not in a solid mass, as in the higher animals, but consist of masses of twisted, ribbon-like tubes.

The blood is a colorless fluid, which does not circulate in closed vessels or veins, but permeates all parts of the body The heart is represented by an elongated, pulsating vessel, situated in the upper part of the body, along the back; it is furnished with small valves, which allow the blood to pass only in one direction, which is toward the head. The blood enters the heart through openings at the sides, and is forced forward and expelled out of an opening in the anterior end; from this it passes backward, through all parts of the body, and again enters the heart, as before. In many naked caterpillars the pulsation of the heart beneath the skin on the back can readily be observed.

Insects do not breath through the mouth or nostrils, as the higher animals do, but through small openings, called

THE INTERNAL ANATOMY OF INSECTS.

spiracles, placed on each side of the body (Fig. 89); these open into minute, pearly tubes (*tracheæ*), which carry the air to all parts of the body, where it comes in contact with the blood. In the perfect or winged insect these tubes are dilated into a great many air-sacs, facilitating their flight.

In many aquatic larvæ—such as those of the Mosquito (Fig. 132)—these tubes project from the body in the form of small tufts, analogous to the gills of fishes. Those insects which, in the perfect state, spend much of their time in the water, are not furnished with these gills, and hence are compelled to rise to the surface of the water occasionally to get air.

Insects (unlike the higher animals) have the skeleton external, or upon the outside, and the muscles are attached to the internal surface of the various parts. The muscles are composed of numerous fibers, which are not united in the rounded, compact form which they have in the higher animals.

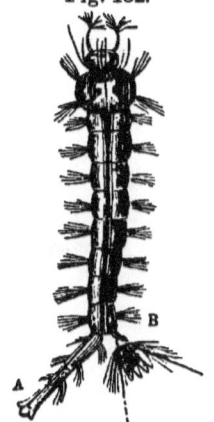

Fig. 132.

No insect is possessed of a voice, and those which appear to sing—such as the Katydids and Crickets—produce their notes by the rubbing together of certain parts of the body. The Cicada, or Harvest-fly, is furnished with a thin, transparent instrument, which is alternately indented and relaxed, producing a sound somewhat similar to that produced by indenting a tin pan.

Some insects produce a shrilling noise by elevating the wing-cases, and rubbing their edges together; others rasp the inside of their hind legs against the outer edges of their wing-cases; some, while on the wing, make a somewhat similar noise by rubbing the front edge of the hind wings against the under side of the wing-cases. Some kinds of Beetles sometimes make a squeaking noise by rubbing the base of the thorax against the adjacent part of the wing-cases.

CHAPTER VIII.

The Seven Orders of Insects.

Naturalist separate insects into seven Orders, characterized by the difference in the mouth parts, and the number and structure of the wings.

These Orders are as follows:

1.—HYMENOPTERA (from two Greek words, meaning *membrane-winged*). Such as Bees, Wasps, Saw Flies, etc.

2.—LEPIDOPTERA (from two Greek words, meaning *scaly-winged*). Such as Butterflies and Moths.

3.—DIPTERA (from two Greek words, signifying *two-winged*). Such as Two-winged Flies, Mosquitoes, etc.

4.—COLEOPTERA (from two Greek words, signifying *sheath-winged*). Such as Beetles and Weevils.

5.—HEMIPTERA (from two Greek words, meaning *half-winged*). Such as Plant Bugs, etc. This Order is divided into two Sub-orders, which are as follows:

Homoptera (from two Greek words, meaning *similar-winged*). Such as Plant-lice, Vine-hoppers, etc.

Heteroptera (from two Greek words, meaning *different-winged*). Such as Plant Bugs, Soldier Bugs, etc.

6.—ORTHOPTERA (from two Greek words, meaning *straight-winged*). Such as Grasshoppers, Crickets, etc.

7.—NEUROPTERA (from two Greek words, meaning *nerve-winged*). Such as Dragon Flies, Lace-winged Flies, etc.

CHAPTER IX.

Classification of Insects into Orders.

By some authors the True Insects are divided into two Sections, as follows:

I. GNAWING INSECTS (*Mandibulata*).—These insects are furnished with a pair of jaws. This Section includes the Orders *Hymenoptera, Coleoptera, Orthoptera,* and *Neuroptera*.

II. SUCKING INSECTS (*Haustellata*).—These insects have the

mouth parts formed into a beak or proboscis. This Section includes the Orders *Lepidoptera*, *Hemiptera*, and *Diptera*.

SECTION 1.—GNAWING IINSECTS (*Mandibulata*).

HYMENOPTERA (*Bees, Wasps, etc.*)—These insects usually have four membranous wings, with few veins, such as the Imported Currant Saw Flies (Fig. 133). The posterior pair are the smallest. The wings are wanting in a few species. The upper jaws are fitted for biting, while the lower jaws form a sheath around the lower lip. The three last named organs are greatly elongated, and fitted for sucking or lapping. The body is usually hard and firm, and in many species the abdomen is furnished with a sting, wherewith the insects defend themselves; some females have an exserted ovipositor (Fig. 129), with which they puncture the

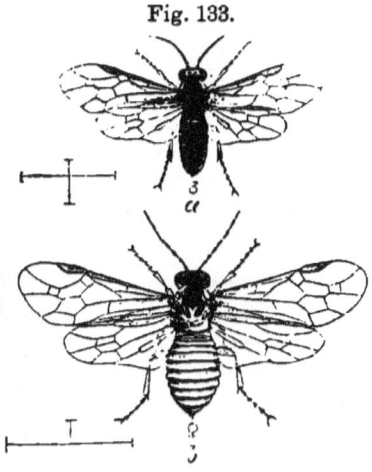

Fig. 133.

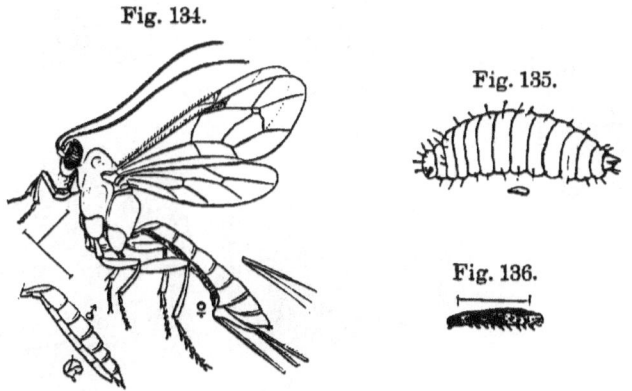

Fig. 134.

Fig. 135.

Fig. 136.

leaves or twigs of plants wherein they deposit their eggs; others, such as the Ichneumon Flies (Figs. 40, 131 and 134) puncture the bodies or eggs of other insects, and deposit their eggs therein. The larva are usually destitute of legs, (like the larva of the Grape Seed Maggot, Fig. 135), and many of them feed upon food provided by the parents; others are provided with twenty or twenty-two legs (such as the larva of the Rose Saw-Fly, Fig. 136), and feed upon the leaves of plants, or live in the stems of plants, or in galls on plants. The transformations are complete, and the legs, etc., of the pupa are enclosed in separate sheaths, (such as the pupa of the Strawberry Saw Fly, Fig. 137, 1 and 2). The larvæ usually pupate in their nests, or in whatever substance they live; others spin cocoons

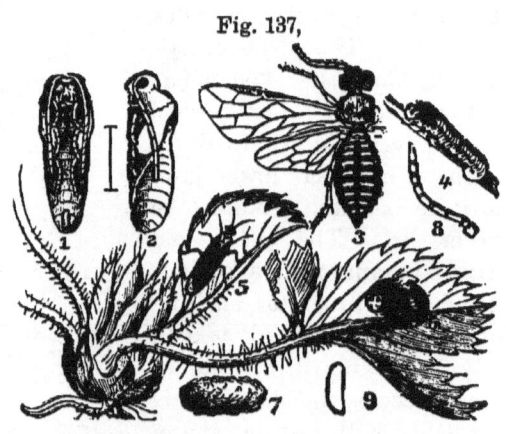

Fig. 137.

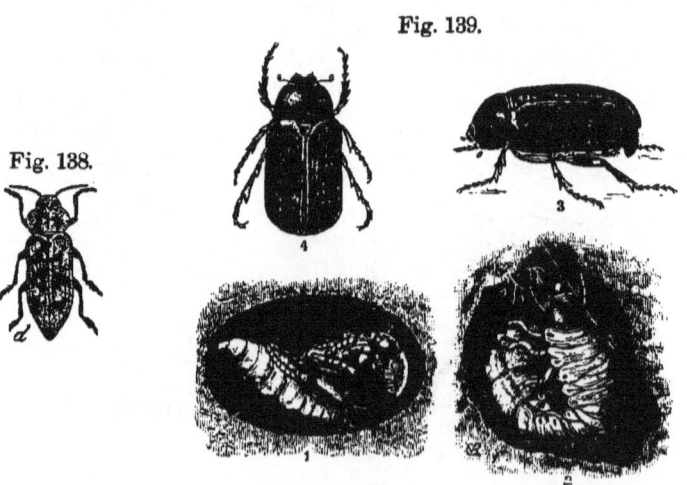

Fig. 138. Fig. 139.

around their bodies, usually first concealing themselves beneath the fallen leaves, or entering the earth.

CLASSIFICATION OF INSECTS INTO ORDERS. 39

COLEOPTERA (*Beetles*).—These insects are usually provided with four wings, but in a few species the hind wings are wanting. The fore wings (*elytra*) are of a hard, horny texture, and meet in a straight line (*suture*) along the back, (except in the genus *Meloe*, where they overlap each other); in a few species they are united at the suture (as in some kinds of Darkling Beetles, Fig. 119). The posterior wings, when present, are membraneous, and when not in use are usually folded both lengthwise and crosswise, and concealed beneath the elytra. (The Beetles which belong to the same family as the Flat-headed Apppple-tree Borer (Fig. 138) have the hind wings folded lengthwise only.) The mouth parts are fitted for biting. Transformations complete.

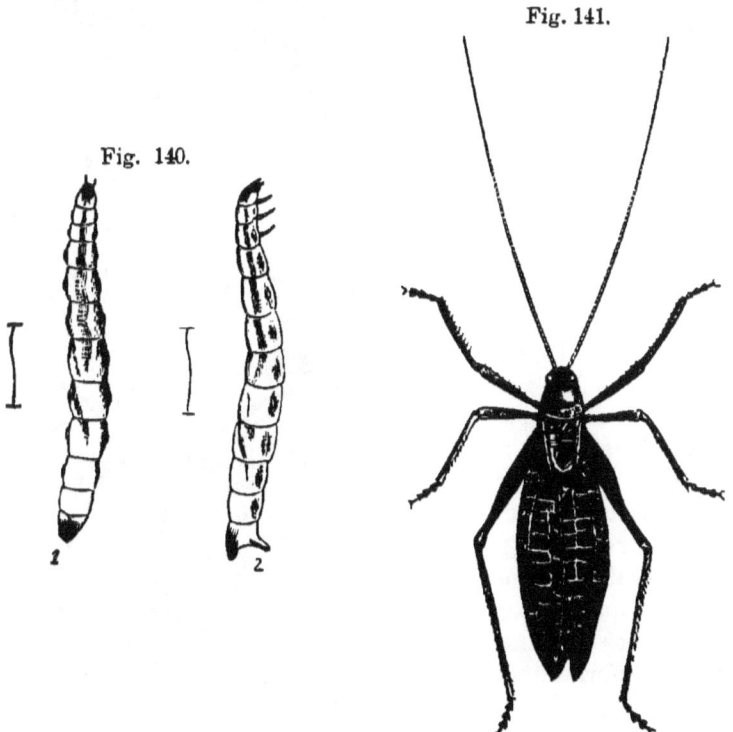

Fig. 140. Fig. 141.

The larvæ are commonly called *grubs*, and are sometimes furnished with six legs, which are placed beneath the fore part of the body (such as the larva of the June Beetle, Fig. 139, 2); besides these some kinds have a fleshy prop-leg beneath the last segment (as the larva of the Striped Cucumber Beetle, Fig. 140). Others are entirely destitute of legs. In all of them the head is distinct. Some undergo their transformations in the substance in which they live; others enter the earth and spin a slight cocoon (Fig. 139, 1). The pupæ have the legs, etc., enclosed in separate sheaths (Fig. 139, 1).

ORTHOPTERA, (*Grasshoppers, Crickets, etc.*) — The insects which belong to this order usually have four wings; the anterior pair are thickened or parchment-like, and overlap each other on the back (as those of the Katydid, Fig. 141), except in the Earwigs (Fig. 41). The posterior wings are thinner, and when at rest are folded up lengthwise, like a fan, and more or less concealed beneath the anterior pair. In a few species one or both pairs of wings are wanting. The mouth parts are fitted for biting. The transformations are incomplete, the pupa being active.

Fig. 142.

With the exception of the insects which belong to the same family as the Mantis (Fig. 142), all the insects belonging to this Order are more or less injurious. In the Earwig family (Fig. 41) the anterior wings meet in a straight line on the back, as in the Rove Beetles (Fig. 249), from which they are at once distinguished by the prominent anal forceps.

Fig. 143.

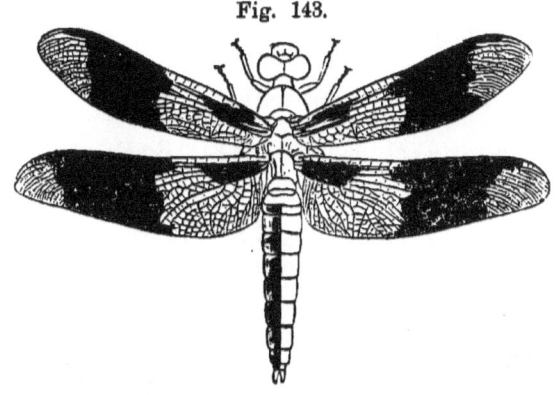

NEUROPTERA (*Dragon Flies, May Flies, etc.*)—These insects are usually provided with four membraneous wings (such as the Dragon Fly, Fig. 143), but in a few species the posterior wings are wanting, while several species are entirely wingless. The wings, when present, are usually provided with numerous cross-veins, forming a network of veins, but in several species (such as in the Genus *Psocus*, Fig. 144), the cross-veins are not more numerous than they are in the wings of Butterflies and Moths. The body and its appendages are usually soft and weak, and the tip of the abdomen is sometimes furnished with two or three long bristles (*setæ*). The mouth parts are fitted for biting. The larvæ are mostly aquatic and are provided with six legs; in some the transformations are incomplete, the pupa being active (as the pupa of the Dragon Fly, Fig. 145); in others they are complete, and the pupa has the legs, etc., enclosed in separate sheaths; several pupæ of the latter kind are active, to a certain extent,

Fig. 144.

Fig. 145.

just before the perfect insect emerges. With the exception of the White Ants, the insects belonging to this Order cannot be regarded as being injurious, while several species are eminently beneficial (such as the Lace-winged Flies, Fig. 22). Some authors have separated those insects belonging to this Order which pass through an incomplete transformation, into a distinct Sub-order, which they call *Pseudo-neuroptera;* but their course has not been very generally followed.

Section 2.—SUCKING INSECTS (*Haustellata*).

Lepidoptera (*Butterflies and Moths*).—These insects are provided with four thin wings, which are usually covered with minute, flattened scales (such as the Semicolon Butterfly, Fig.

Fig. 146.

146, and the Orchard Tent-caterpillar Moth, Fig. 147);* the females of a few species are either wingless (as the female of the Yellow Canker-worm Moth, Fig. 148), or the wings are small

Fig. 147.   Fig. 148.

and rudimentary. The body and its appendages are also covered with scales or short hairs. The mouth parts are fitted for

---

*The antennæ of Butterflies always terminate in a knob (see Figs. 95 and 146); but the antennæ of Moths never terminate in a knob (see Figs. 97, 115, *a*, and 147).

sucking, the upper lip and jaws being very small or rudimentary, while the lower jaws are formed into a long tube or proboscis, which, when not in use, is coiled up like the hair spring of a watch (Fig. 115, *g*,) and concealed beneath the head; in a few species which take no food while in the perfect state, the lower jaws are also rudimentary. The transformations are complete, and the various members of the pupa are enclosed in a common sheath or covering (as the pupa of the Achemon Sphinx, Fig. 149). A few of the larvæ of the smaller species of Moths are destitute of legs; others are provided with ten legs (as the Spring Canker Worm, Fig. 150, *a*);

Fig. 149.

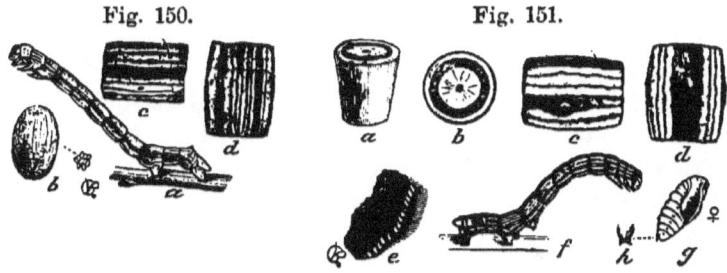

Fig. 150.   Fig. 151.

some with twelve legs (as the Fall Canker Worm, Fig. 151, *f*); the greater number have sixteen legs (as the larva of the Achemon Sphinx, Fig. 152); while a few of small size, which

Fig. 152.

mine the leaves of plants, have more than sixteen legs; in all of them the head is distinct. They are all more or less injurious, with the single exception of one species (the *Dakruma coccidivorella* of Comstock) which feeds upon young Scale-insects.

HEMIPTERA (*True Bugs*).—These insects are usually provided with four wings, but a few kinds have only two, while others are entirely destitute of wings. The mouth is fitted for suction, and is commonly called the "beak," or "proboscis." (See the Dotted-legged Plant-bug, Fig. 20, *c;* the Spined Soldier Bug, Fig. 114, *a;* the Ring Banded Soldier Bug, Fig. 153, *c;*

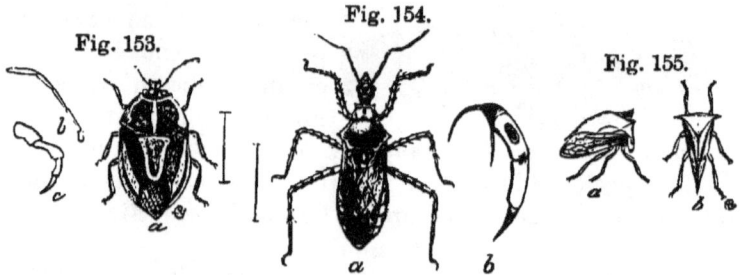

Fig. 153. Fig. 154. Fig. 155.

and the Many Banded Robber, Fig. 154, *b*.) It usually consists of four bristle-like organs (the upper and the lower jaws), which are inclosed in the sheath-like lower lip; the upper lip is short and pointed. The transformations are incomplete. This Order is divided into two Sub-orders, as follows:

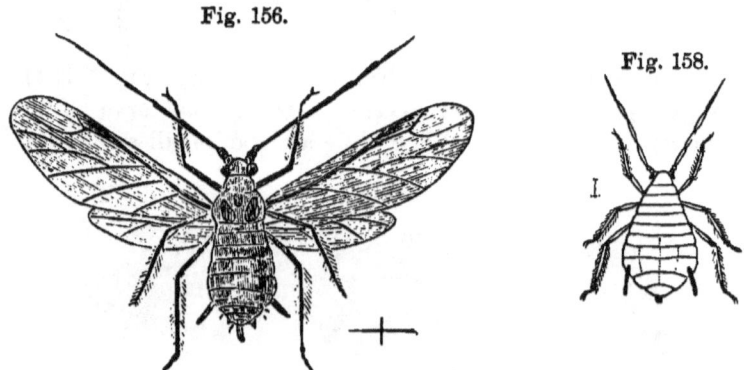

Fig. 156. Fig. 158.

Homoptera (Plant-lice, Vine-hoppers, etc).—These insects have the wings of the same texture throughout, either wholly leathery (as those of the Buffalo Tree-hopper, Fig. 155), or wholly membraneous (as those of the Grain Aphis, Fig. 156), and when at rest they are held slanting over the back like a

CLASSIFICATION OF INSECTS INTO ORDERS. 45

steep roof (as in the Hop Aphis, Fig. 157, 2); the beak arises from the posterior part of the under side of the head, and sometimes apparently from the breast.

They are all terrestrial, and are injurious to vegetation. Many of them are wingless (as in Fig. 157, 4, and the Apple Tree Aphis, Fig. 158). In one family—the Scale-insects—

Fig. 157.

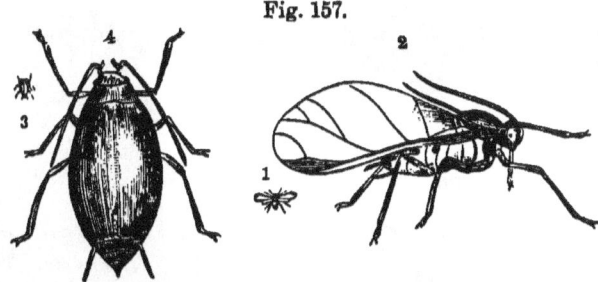

the females (such as those of the Red Scale, Fig. 159, *1b*,) are wingless, and the males are provided with only two wings (Fig. 159, *1a*).

Fig. 159.

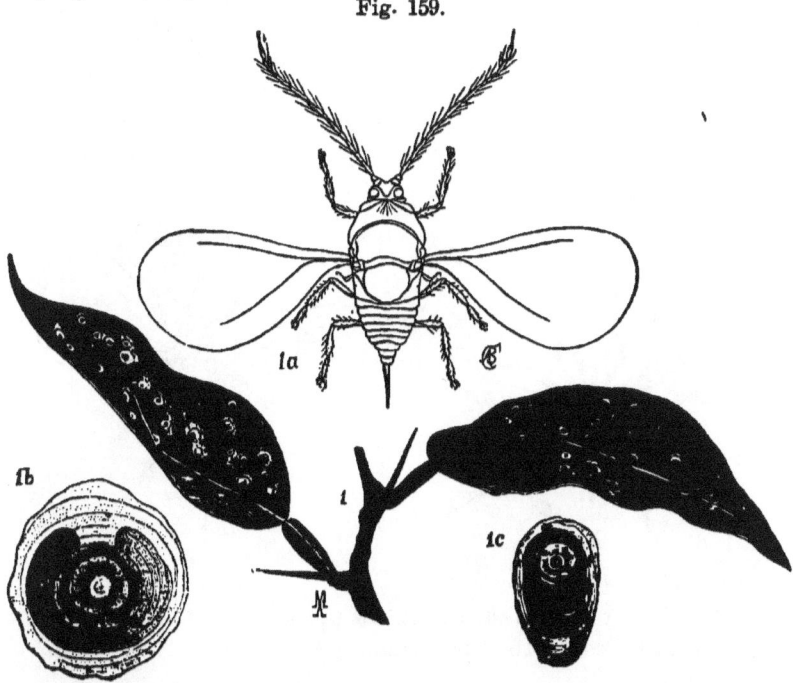

Heteroptera (Plant Bugs, Soldier Bugs, etc.).—These insects have the anterior wings thickened at the base, while the outer part is thin and more membraneous (such as those of the Harlequin Cabbage Bug, Fig. 160). When at rest they lie flatly

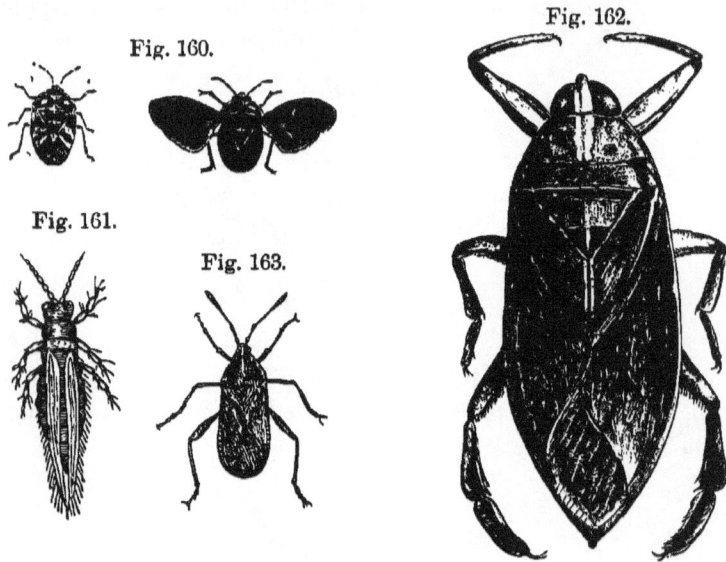

upon the back, and overlap each other at the tips. The beak issues from the fore part of the under side of the head, while

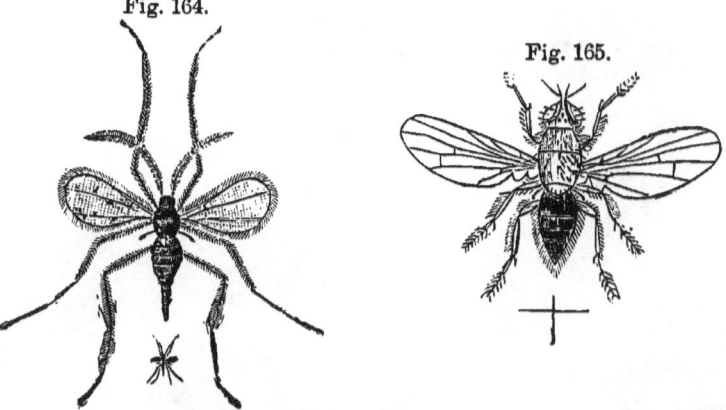

in the Homoptera it issues from the posterior part of the under side of the head. In a few small species, such as the Thrips

(Fig. 161) and the wingless Lice, the mouth is furnished with jaws. Some of the insects which belong to this sub-order are terrestrial, others are aquatic (as the Large Belostoma, Fig. 162). A very few species are predaceous; others are parasitic, while still others feed upon the juices of various plants (such as the Squash Bug, Fig. 163).

DIPTERA (*Two-winged Flies*).—These insects are provided with only two wings, the posterior pair being represented by a pair of thread-like organs, knobbed at the outer end (such as those of the Wheat Midge, Fig. 164, and the Onion Fly, Fig. 165). These are called *balancers*, or *halteres*, and are never wanting, even in those species which are wingless. The mouth parts are fitted for piercing or lapping. Transformations complete. The larvæ are destitute of legs (such as the Apple Maggot, Fig. 166, and the larvæ of the Helophilus Fly, Fig. 167),

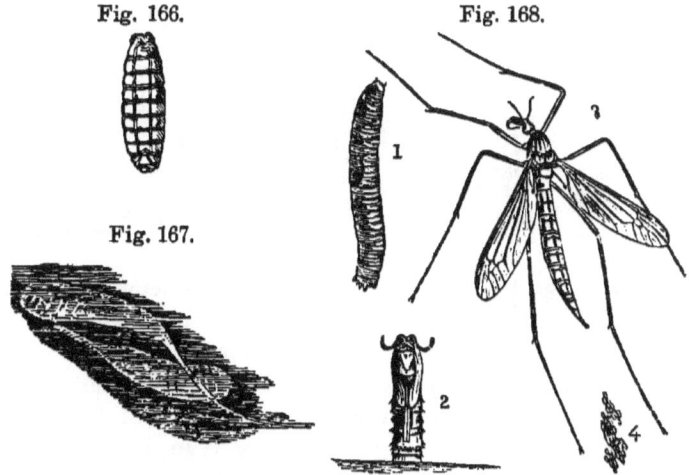

Fig. 166.

Fig. 168.

Fig. 167.

and are commonly called "maggots;" some are furnished with a distinct head (as the larva of the Crane Fly, Fig. 168, 1), while in others this part is soft, and of no definite shape. The legs, etc., of the pupa (Fig. 168, 2,) are confined in separate sheaths, but the entire pupa is sometimes inclosed in the hardened skin of the larva (as the pupa of the Apple Maggot, Fig. 76).

CHAPTER X.

Classification of Larvæ.

Those insects which, when they first issue from the egg, closely resemble the parents, are always provided with six legs. Those which are furnished with a beak belong to the Order Hemiptera, such as the larva of the Cabbage Bug (Fig. 66, a), and the larva of the Soldier Bug (Fig. 43, b). Those which are provided with jaws belong either to the Orthoptera or the Neuroptera; if aquatic, they belong to the latter order; but if terrestrial, they belong to Orthoptera, such as the larva of the Earwig (Fig. 41, a). Those which are worm-like when they issue from the egg, and are destitute of legs—such as those which are commonly called "maggots" or "grubs,"—

Fig. 169.

belong either to the Order Coleoptera, Hymenoptera, or Diptera. If the body is flattened, like the larva of the Broad-necked Prionus (Fig. 169), the larva belongs to the Coleoptera, and is probably the larva of a Long-horned Borer, or of a Saw-horned Borer; if they live in nests stored with dead insects or with pollen, they belong to the Order Hymenoptera; if they have a soft, retractile head, of no definite shape, they belong to the Order Diptera, as the larva of the Ox Bot-fly (Fig. 170.) In the Lepidopterous families *Lycænidæ* and *Bombycidæ*, a few larvæ have the legs so small as to be scarcely distinguishable; these larvæ, or caterpillars, live exposed upon the leaves of plants and trees.

Those larvæ which are worm-like and provided with six legs, such as those which are commonly called "grubs," as the larva of the Asparagus Beetle (Fig. 171) and the larva of

CLASSIFICATION OF LARVÆ.

the Rove Beetle (Fig. 172)—belong either to the Order Coleoptera or Neuroptera. If they are terrestrial they probably belong to the Order Coleoptera, the only Neuropterous larvæ which are terrestrial being those of the Lace-winged Flies (Fig. 47), and of the Ant Lions. These larvæ differ from the Coleopterous larvæ by their long and prominent jaws, which project horizontally in front of the head.

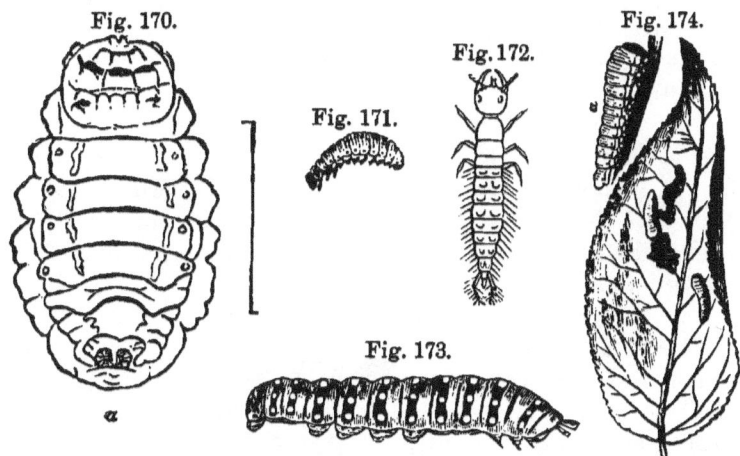

Fig. 170. Fig. 171. Fig. 172. Fig. 173. Fig. 174.

Those larvæ which are provided with from ten to sixteen legs, such as are commonly called "Caterpillars," (as the Parsley Worm, Fig. 173), "Span Worms," "Measuring Worms," etc., belong to the Order Lepidoptera.

Those larvæ which are provided with more than sixteen legs are called "False Caterpillars," such as the Pear Slug (Fig. 174); they belong to the Order Hymenoptera, and to the family of Saw Flies.

CHAPTER XI.

Classification of Insects.

Insects are divided into orders, orders into families, families into genera, genera into species.

Or to reverse this and illustrate: The Southern Cabbage Butterfly (Fig. 175) is a species, and the Imported Cabbage Butterfly (Fig. 176) is another species. These, with other species of a similar form, though not of the same color, form a *genus*.

The common Yellow Butterflies form another genus. These and several other genera, agreeing in certain respects, form a family. This and several other families of Butterflies, Sphinx Moths, Night Flying Moths, etc., all agreeing in certain respects (for instance, in having scaly wings and bodies) form the Order *Lepidoptera*.

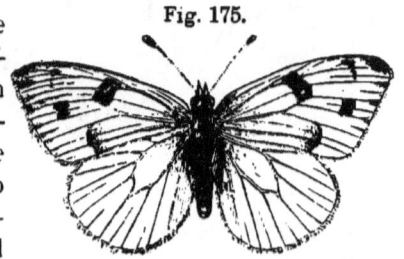

Fig. 175.

As a general rule, all the species of a family have sufficient resemblance to each other to enable even unscientific persons, by a little study and observation, to associate them with reasonable correctness, and among insects they usually have somewhat similar habits, so that knowing the habits of a given family, when we find a species belonging to it, we have a pretty correct idea of its habits.

As illustrating the method of ascertaining the Order to which any perfect insect belongs, supposing an insect is presented with the inquiry: To what Order does it belong? On examination, if it is found to have biting jaws, it belongs to the gnawing insects (*Mandibulata*), and therefore must either belong to the Order Hymenoptera, Coleoptera, Orthoptera, or Neuroptera, as these are the only insects having biting jaws. If the fore or upper wings are of a hard and horny texture, and the under wings are thin and membraneous, and folded both lengthwise and crosswise, the insect is a Beetle, (as the

Prickly Bark Beetle Fig. 177), and therefore belongs to the Order Coleoptera, as this is the only order of insects having biting jaws, and wings of the kind described above. If the fore or upper wings are parchment-like, or leathery, and the under wings membraneous and folded lengthwise like a fan, (as those of the Katydid Fig. 141), the insect belongs to the Order Orthoptera, as this is the only order of insects having biting jaws and wings of the kind described above.

Fig. 176.

Fig. 177.

If the insect is provided with four wings, all of which are thin and membraneous, and is furnished with biting jaws, it belongs either to the Hymenoptera or Neuroptera. If the abdomen is provided with a sting or piercer (as that of the Wasp or Hornet, Fig. 1), it belongs to the Order Hymenoptera, as this is the only order of insects having biting jaws and four membraneous wings, that has the abdomen armed with a sting or piercer. But if the four wings are of equal size, and crossed by numerous veins, forming a net-like structure, and the abdomen is soft and not armed with a sting (such as the Dragon Fly, Fig. 143), the insect belongs to the Order Neuroptera, as this is the only order of insects having biting jaws and four wings of equal size, and the abdomen not armed with a sting.

Supposing the insect presented has a mouth formed for sucking (as the Tomato Worm Moth, Fig. 178), then it belongs either to the Order Lepidoptera, Hemiptera, or Diptera—the *Haustellate* Orders. If it is provided with four wings covered with scales, and the mouth parts formed for sucking (as in Fig. 178), it belongs to the Order Lepidoptera, as this is the only order of insects having four wings covered with scales, and a a mouth formed for sucking.

If the mouth parts are formed for sucking, and in the form of a beak (as in the Dotted Legged Plant-bug, Fig. 20), and the insect is provided with four wings, it belongs to the Order

Fig. 178.

Hemiptera, which is divided into two Sub-orders—Homoptera and Heteroptera.

If the beak issues from the anterior part of the under side

of the head, and the fore or upper wings are thicker at the base than at the tip or apex, and lie flatly on the back, overlapping each other (as those of the Spined Soldier Bug, Fig. 114), the insect belongs to the Sub-order Heteroptera.

But if the beak issues from the posterior part of the under side of the head, and the anterior wings are of the same texture throughout, and when at rest are held over the back like a steep roof (as those of the Hop Aphis, Fig. 157, 2), the insect belongs to the Sub-order Homoptera.

If the insect is provided with only two wings, and the mouth parts are formed for sucking (as the Horse Bot Fly, Fig. 179), it belongs to the Order Diptera, as this is the only order of insects which has only two wings, and the mouth parts formed for sucking or lapping.

Fig. 179.

The Fleas were formerly regarded as comprising a distinct Order, called *Aphaniptera*, but most modern authors class them with the Diptera.

Bedbugs are placed in the Order Hemiptera, as their mouth parts are beak-like.

The Head and Body-lice are also placed in the Order Hemiptera, since their mouth parts form a beak-like sucker. Chicken-lice, and those infesting fowls and animals, although they have biting jaws, are placed in the Order Hemiptera, and seem to connect this order with the Orthoptera.

There are wingless insects belonging to nearly every Order of insects, but these can generally be easily classified by the structure of their mouth parts.

The names of the different Orders end in *ptera* (meaning *wing*), as Coleo*ptera*, Dip*tera*, etc.; while the names of the Families terminate in *idæ* (meaning *like* or *similar*) as Carab*idæ*, Buprest*idæ*, etc.

In writing the scientific or technical name of an insect, the *generic* name, or name of the genus, is written first, followed by its *specific* name, or name of the species; attached to this is usually the name of the person who first named and described the species; and if any person named and described the same species afterward, the name the latter gave it is called a synonym of the name given it by its first describer. In some cases the first describer of a species placed the latter in the wrong genus; but when the species is restored to its proper genus, the name of its first describer (and not the name of the person who first referred it to its proper genus), must still be attached to the specific name. In cases of this kind most writers of the present day enclose the name of the first describer in a parenthesis ( ). The following example will serve to illustrate this:

(Generic name.)   (Specific name.)   (First describer.)
PHILAMPELIS   ACHEMON   (Drury).

Synonyms.   *Sphinx achemon.* Drury.
            Sphinx crantor. Cramer.

This insect was first described by Mr. Drury, who named it *Sphinx achemon*; but as it belongs to the genus *Philampelis* instead of to *Sphinx*, it is now known as *Philampelis achemon* (Drury). A few years after Mr. Drury described it, Mr. Cramer, supposing it to be an undescribed species, described it under the name of *Sphinx crantor*, which thus becomes a synonym of the name given this insect by Mr. Drury.

CHAPTER XII.

Classification of Insects into Families.

It is a pretty well established fact that all the members of any given Family of insects, almost without exception, have similar habits; so that by being able to refer any insect to its proper Family, we can usually tell whether it is an injurious or a beneficial insect, according to the habits of the other insects which belong to the same Family.

ORDER I. HYMENOPTERA. (*Bees, Wasps, etc.*)

The following are the principal Families of this extensive Order:

BEES (*Apidæ*).—These insects have the antennæ from

twelve to thirteen jointed; the tongue and other mouth parts are usually very long, and the posterior tibiæ, and sometimes the basal joint of the posterior feet, are broad, and in some species there is a bristly cavity on each posterior tibia in which these insects, such as the Honey Bees, carry pollen, etc., to their nests. Some kinds construct nests of mud; others burrow into the stems of plants, into soft or decayed wood, or into the ground, such as the Bumble Bees (Fig. 180). A few kinds line their nests with pieces of green leaves, such as the Leaf-cutting Bee. The larvæ of a few species live parasitically in the nests of pollen-gathering Bees, and subsist upon the food which had been stored up

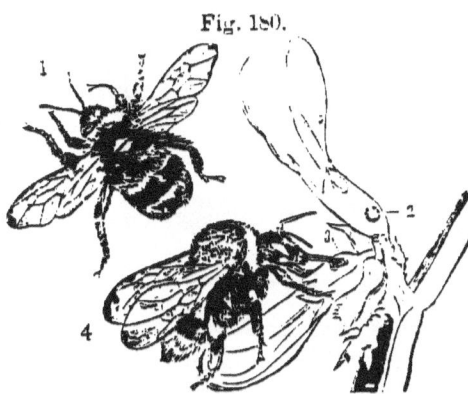

Fig. 180.

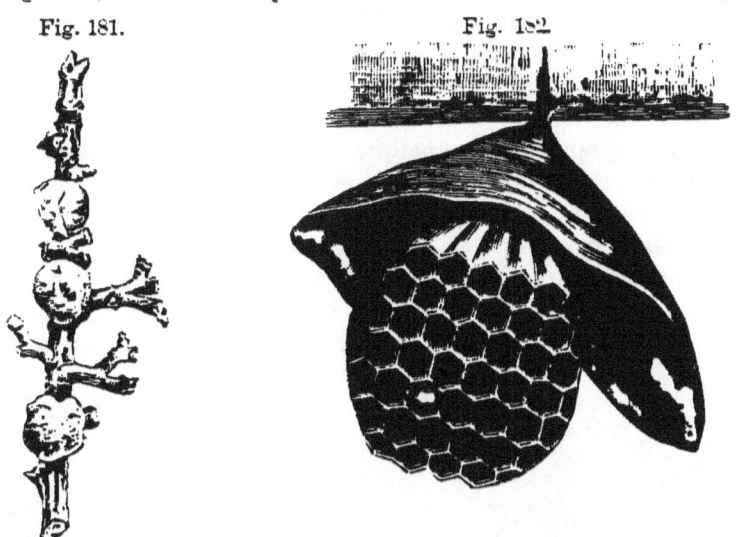

Fig. 181. Fig. 182.

for the young of the latter; on this account they are commonly called "Cuckoo Bees." The larvæ belonging to this

Family are wholly destitute of feet, like the larva of the Grape Seed Maggot (Fig. 135).

WASPS (*Vespidæ*). These insects have the body hard and smooth; the antennæ are elbowed (*geniculate*); the wings are folded lengthwise once when at rest, and the hind legs are smooth. These insects build nests either of mud (Fig. 181),

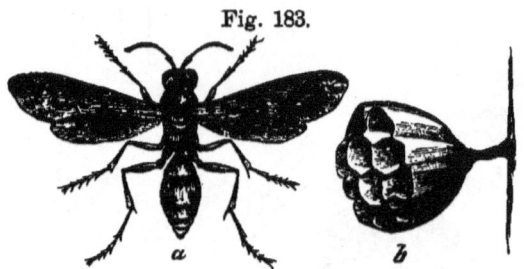

Fig. 183.

or of a papery substance (Figs. 182 and 183, *b*), and store them with small caterpillars or other larvæ, or with a pulpy mass composed of the bodies of other insects chewed up into a pulp. Many of these wasps are predaceous, such as the Rust Red Wasp (Fig. 183, *a*), feeding upon flies, etc., but some species attack ripe fruit. The larvæ are destitute of feet, and feed upon the food stored up by the parents.

SAND WASPS OR WOOD WASPS (*Crabronidæ, Nyssonidæ, Bembecidæ, etc.*).—These insects usually have large heads, and the antennæ are sometimes elbowed. They build their nests in holes in wood, in the stems of plants, or in the earth, and store them with spiders, flies, plant-lice, etc. The larvæ are destitute of legs, and feed upon the food stored up by the parent insects.

DIGGER WASPS (*Pompilidæ, etc.*). These Wasps have long and usually spiny legs and large jaws; the antennæ are not elbowed, and the abdomen is petiolate. They build their nests in holes which they dig in the earth, storing them with insects and spiders. A few kinds are known to feed upon over-ripe fruit, such as the Red-winged

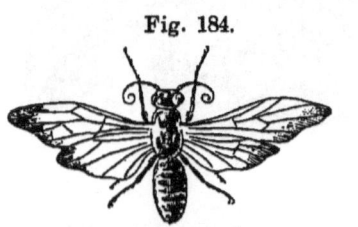

Fig. 184.

Wasp (Fig. 184). The larvæ are destitute of feet. A large species of this Family is commonly called the "Tarantula Hawk."

ANTS (*Formicidæ*).—The males and females, when they first issue from the pupa, are usually provided with four wings, but the workers are wingless; the antennæ are always elbowed. The larvæ are footless, and are fed upon food which has been elaborated in the stomachs of the workers.

GOLDEN WASPS (*Chrysididæ*).—These insects are either green or black; the antennæ are elbowed and composed of thirteen joints; the eyes are oval, and the ocelli are distinct. The larvæ are destitute of feet, and live in the nests of Bees or Wasps, first destroying the original inhabitant, and then feeding upon the food that had been stored up for it.

ICHNEUMON FLIES (*Ichneumonidæ*).—These insects have the antennæ long and composed of from fifteen to fifty joints, as the Ring Legged Pimpla (Fig. 134) and the Delicate Long Sting (Fig. 131), and are not usually elbowed; the abdomen is usually long and slender (Fig. 131), the ovipositor is sometimes exserted, and is frequently as long and occasionally much longer than the body (Fig. 131). These insects are among the most beneficial insects known, as their larvæ live within the bodies of caterpillars and other injurious larvæ (as the Bracon Fly parasite, Fig. 185, which preys upon De Long's Moth), as well as in the bodies of many perfect insects, spiders, etc., ultimately causing their death. The larvæ are footless, and usually spin cocoons wherein to undergo their transformations.

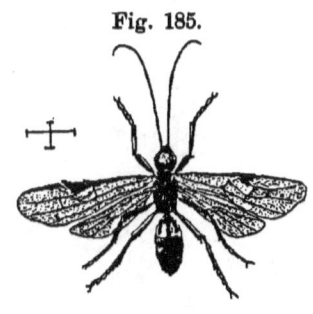

Fig. 185.

EGG PARASITES (*Proctotrupidæ*).—These are minute insects with only a few veins in the wings (Fig. 186), frequently only one, and the antennæ are sometimes elbowed; the ovipositor of the female issues from the tip of the abdomen. They live in the larval state within the eggs, larvæ or pupæ of other insects. The perfect insects seldom exceed one twenty-eighth of an inch in length.

BRASSLETS OR CHALCIS FLIES (*Chalcididæ*).—These are very small insects with elbowed antennæ (as shown in Fig. 187), and frequently of a metallic color; the wings are usually furnished

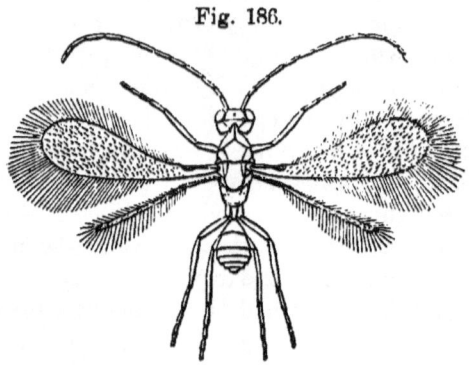

Fig. 186.

with but few veins (Fig. 188), sometimes only one, while a few species are destitute of wings; the ovipositor of the female issues from the underside of the abdomen forward of the tip. The larvæ are footless, and live in the eggs, larvæ or pupæ of other insects, while a few kinds live in galls or in fruits; they do not usually spin cocoons before assuming the pupa form.

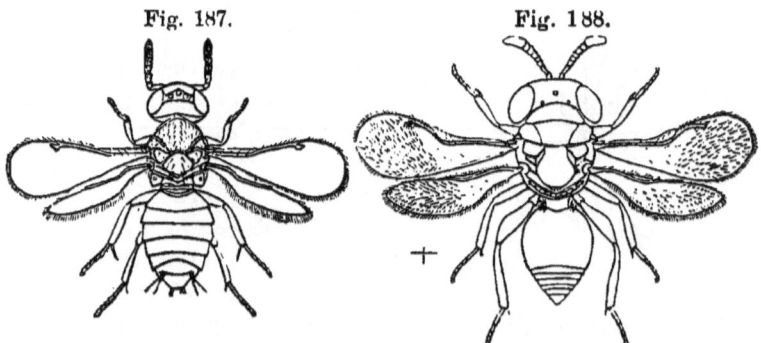

Fig. 187. Fig. 188.

GALL FLIES (*Cynipidæ*).—These insects have the antennæ composed of from thirteen to sixteen joints, and not elbowed; the abdomen of the female is usually armed with a piercer. The larvæ live in galls on plants, or in the larvæ or pupæ of other insects.

SAW FLIES (*Tenthredinidæ*).—In these insects the veins of the fore wings extend to the outer margin; the antennæ are not elbowed, as in the Native Currant Saw-fly (Fig. 189), the

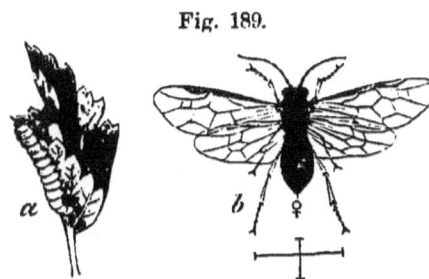

Fig. 189.

anterior tibiæ have two spurs at the tip of each; the abdomen is united to the thorax by nearly its whole width, the segments of the abdomen are nearly of the same width, and the abdomen of the female is furnished with two saw-like instruments (Fig. 129), with which she punctures the leaves or tender stems of plants, where the eggs are deposited. The larvæ are usually naked, and are provided with twenty or twenty-two legs (Figs. 44, 60, 136, 137 and 174). They usually live exposed upon the leaves of plants, but a few kinds live in galls. (For other examples of the perfect insects see Figs. 15, 130 and 133.)

HORN TAILS (*Uroceridæ*).—These insects are usually of a large size; the veins of the front wings extend to the outer edge; the abdomen is more or less cylindrical, and in the males there is a long horn at the tip; the ovipositor of the female is attached to the middle of the underside of the abdomen, and extends far beyond its tip, and the anterior tibiæ have a single spur at the tip. The larvæ live in the trunks, etc., of trees, and are provided with only six legs, the pro-legs being obsolete, or nearly so.

CHAPTER XIII.

Order II. LEPIDOPTERA. (*Butterflies and Moths.*)

The insects belonging to this Order are divided into two Sections, as follows:

Section I.—Butterflies (*Rhopalocera*).—In these insects the antennæ are filiform and terminate in a knob (Fig. 95), which is sometimes produced into a hook at the tip.

These insects fly only in the day time, and are usually arrayed in bright colors; the hind wings are generally colored as brightly as the fore ones; when at rest the wings are usually brought together over the back, but some of the Skippers hold the hind wing stretched out or expanded when at rest. The larvæ or caterpillars mostly live exposed upon the leaves of plants, but a few kinds live under a web, in a rolled leaf, or in a nest formed by fastening several leaves together with silken threads. They are provided with sixteen legs, but in a few kinds these are so small that in creeping the whole under surface of the body touches the object upon which the caterpillar is crawling.

When about to assume the pupa form, the greater number suspend themselves in various ways; others construct a sort of cocoon by fastening several leaves together with silken threads, and lining the interior with a thin layer of silk.

The chrysalids of this latter class are usually smooth and cylindrical, but taper posteriorly; the others are angular and more or less tuberculate.

Section II.—Moths (*Heterocera*).—In these insects the antennæ never terminate in a knob, although it is frequently thickened toward the tip.

These insects usually fly about only at night or in the evening; their colors are usually dull, mostly some shade of gray, and the hind wings are seldom colored as brightly as the fore ones, being usually of a dirty white or smoky color. When at rest the wings usually cover the back like a steep roof, the fore wings concealing the hind ones.

A very few of the caterpillars (such as those of the Plume Moths) suspend themselves when about to pupate; but the greater number either spin cocoons, or enter the earth and form smooth cells in which to undergo their transformations.

SECTION I.—BUTTERFLIES. (*Rhopalocera.*)

These insects are divided into five Families, as follows:

SWALLOW-TAILS (*Papilionidæ*).—These Butterflies have the hind wings produced into a broad tail, and are hollowed out next the body (as the Turnus Butterfly, Fig. 190); the anterior pair of tibiæ have a stout spur near the middle of each.

Fig. 190.

These Butterflies are usually of a large size, and the colors are mostly yellow and black.

Their caterpillars live exposed upon the leaves (such as the caterpillar of the Turnus Butterfly, Fig. 49), sometimes spinning a web upon the upper surface of a leaf, upon which they rest when not feeding. When about to pupate they suspend themselves by the hind part of the body, and a transverse loop of silken threads passed around the fore part of the body.

WHITE AND YELLOW BUTTERFLIES (*Pieridæ*).—These Butterflies have the hind wings rounded behind, or not tailed, and the inner margin is concave; the anterior tibiæ are destitute of a spur at the middle; the colors are white and black (as those of the Imported Cabbage Butterfly, Fig. 191), or yellow and black, sometimes tinged with green. Their caterpillars live exposed on the leaves (as those of the Imported Cabbage Butterfly, Fig. 192, *a*), and when about to pupate they suspend themselves by the hind part of the body and a transverse loop of silken threads (Fig. 192, *b*). They are generally naked or nearly so, and the color is usually green.

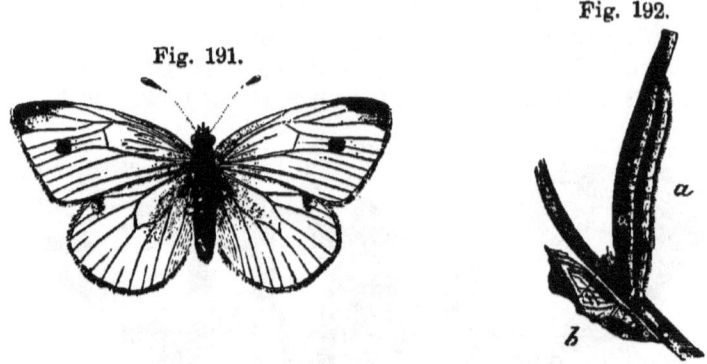

Fig. 191. Fig. 192.

FOUR-FOOTED BUTTERFLIES (*Nymphalidæ*).—These Butterflies usually have the hind wings rounded (as the Tawny Emperor Butterfly, Fig. 193, *d*), and the first pair of feet are

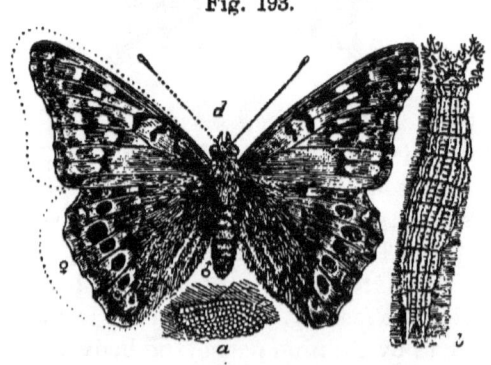

Fig. 193.

imperfect, being destitute of claws, and are never used in walking; the first pair of legs are folded up against the breast, like a tippet. The colors are usually brown and black, sometimes almost wholly black, or marked with whitish bands or borders.

Their caterpillars are sometimes naked (as the caterpillar

of the Archippus Butterfly, Fig. 78), but are more often covered with spines or bristles; they usually live exposed upon the leaves, but several kinds live beneath a web. When about to pupate they suspend themselves by the hind part of the body (Figs. 79 and 80). The Archippus Butterfly (Fig. 81) belongs to this Family.

THECLA AND COPPER BUTTERFLIES (*Lycænidæ*).—These are small butterflies of a blue, brown or black color, and in a few species the hind wings are furnished with one or two very slender tails; the hind wings are hollowed out next the body, and the hind tibiæ are furnished with only one pair of spurs.

Their caterpillars live exposed upon the leaves of plants, and are usually naked, of a green color, and nearly destitute of feet. When about to pupate they suspend themselves by the hind part of the body, and a transverse loop of silken threads passed around the fore part of the body.

Fig. 194.

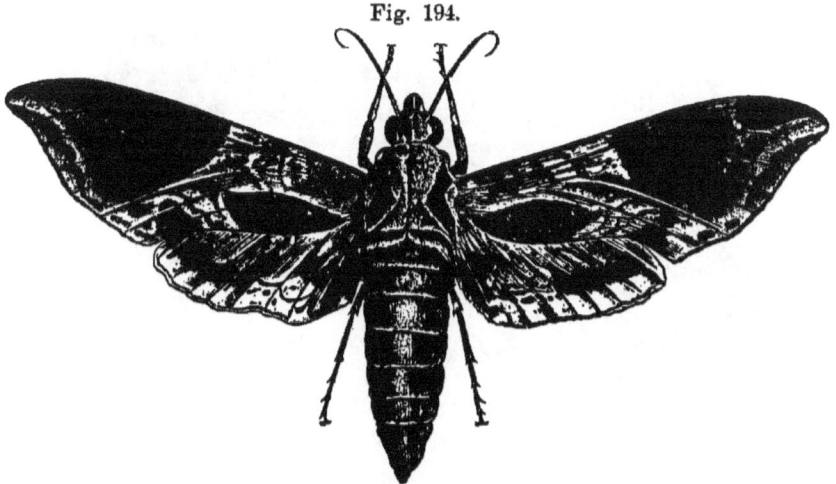

SKIPPERS (*Hesperidæ*).—These Butterflies have large heads and thick bodies; when at rest the hind wings are usually spread out, while the fore ones are brought together over the back; the middle tibiæ are furnished with a pair of spurs near the middle of each, and the hind tibiæ usually have a pair of spurs at the middle and another pair at the tips; the claws at the end of the feet have a deep notch in the middle.

64 NATURAL HISTORY OF INSECTS.

These insects fly with a rapid, jerking motion; the colors are mostly black and brown.

Their caterpillars are usually naked and spindle shaped, with the head much wider than the fore part of the first segment of the body; they usually live between two or more leaves fastened together with silken threads. They pupate in their cases, and the chrysalids are smooth and taper at one end, and are usually covered with a bluish powder.

SECTION II.—MOTHS. (*Heterocera*.)

These insects are divided into nine Families, as follows:

HAWK-MOTHS (*Sphingidæ*).—These moths have the body stout and spindle shaped; the wings are strong, long and narrow, and sometimes partly transparent; the hind wings are usually not more than one half as long as the fore wings; the

Fig. 195.

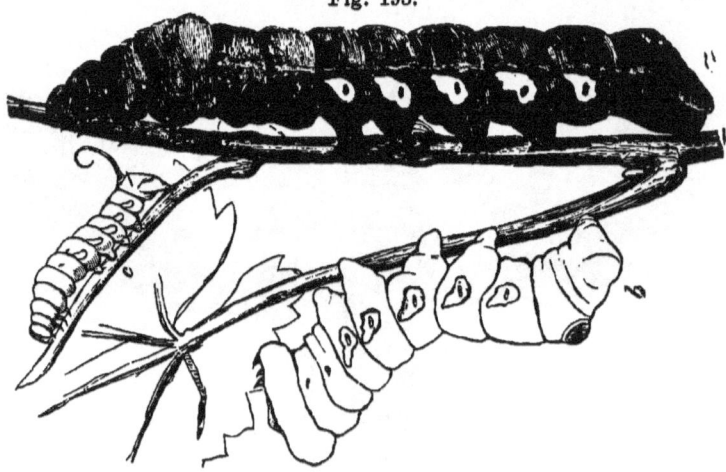

head is not sunken into the thorax; the palpi are very stout and hairy, and are placed close together; the antennæ are usually prismatic and spindle-shaped, and are sometimes hooked at the tip.

These moths fly mostly in the evening twilight; their flight is strong and rapid, and they may frequently be seen hovering over flowers, like a humming-bird.

Their caterpillars are naked and provided with sixteen legs, and sometimes have a spine or horn on the eleventh segment;

Fig. 196.

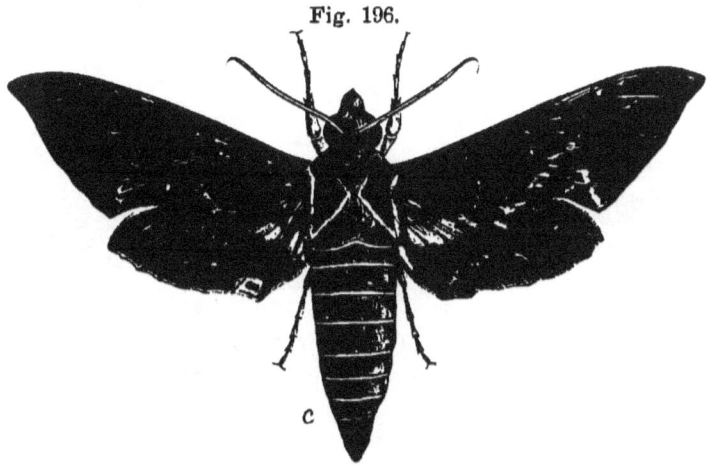

c

they live exposed upon the leaves of plants. When about to pupate they either creep beneath the fallen leaves, etc., or else enter the earth and form smooth cells in which to undergo

Fig. 197.

their transformations. The Satellitia Sphinx and Caterpillar (Figs. 194 and 195), the Achemon Sphinx and Caterpillar (Figs. 196 and 152), and the White-lined Sphinx and Caterpillar (Figs. 197 and 198), are examples of this Family.

CLEAR-WINGED MOTHS (*Ægeridæ*).—These insects have the body quite slender, and there is frequently a fan-shaped tuft at the tip; the wings are narrow and usually partially transparent, and the hind wings are nearly as long as the front ones.

Fig. 198

These insects are diurnal in their habits, and quite closely resemble certain wasps, but the body is clothed with scales, and is not pointed behind.

Their caterpillars are provided with sixteen legs, and usually live within the stems or roots of plants; they pupate within their burrows. The Peach-tree Borer and Moth (Figs. 199 and 200), and the Raspberry Borer (Fig. 201) are examples of this Family.

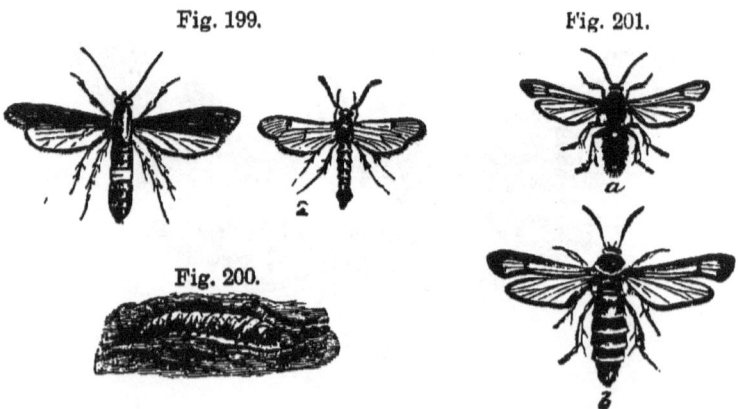

Fig. 199. Fig. 201. Fig. 200.

WOOD NYMPHS (*Zygænidæ*).—In these insects the head is not sunken into the thorax, the palpi are slender, the wings are quite long and narrow, and the thorax is not tufted. The ground color is usually black or white.

The larvæ are provided with sixteen legs, and are usually

CLASSIFICATION OF INSECTS INTO FAMILIES.   67

naked, but are sometimes more or less covered with hairs. Some kinds spin cocoons when about to pupate, but the greater number enter the earth, or burrow into soft wood, and form cells in which to undergo their transformations. The

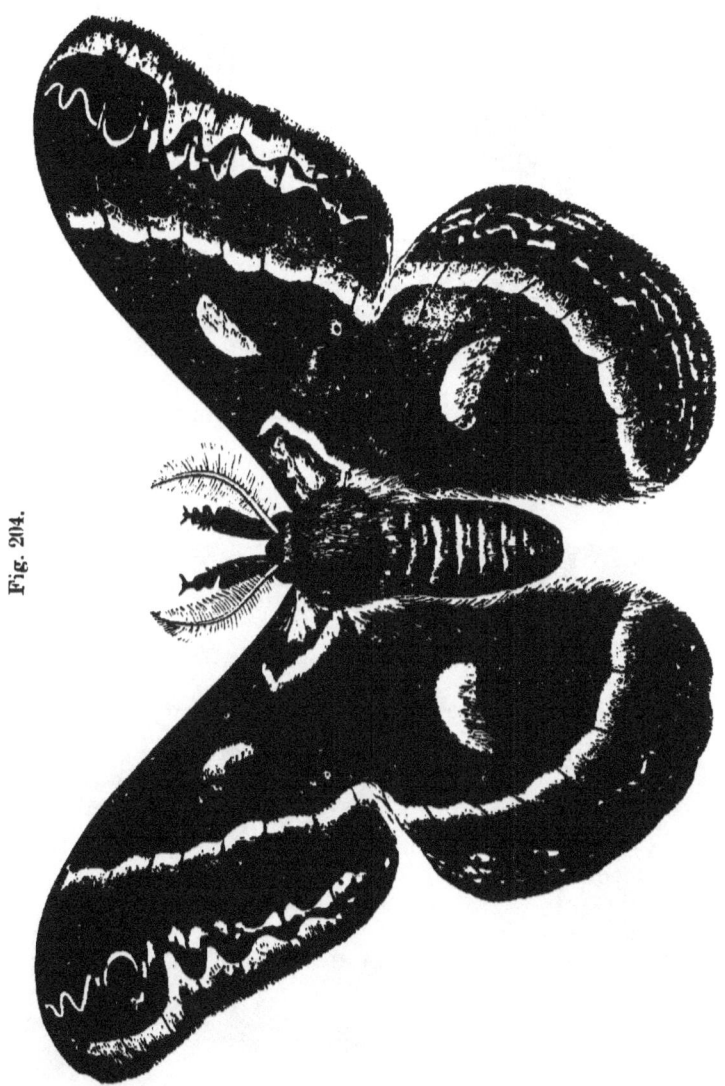

Fig. 204.

Beautiful Wood Nymph (Fig. 17); the Eight Spotted Forester (Fig. 202), and the American Procris (Fig. 203), are excellent examples of this Family.

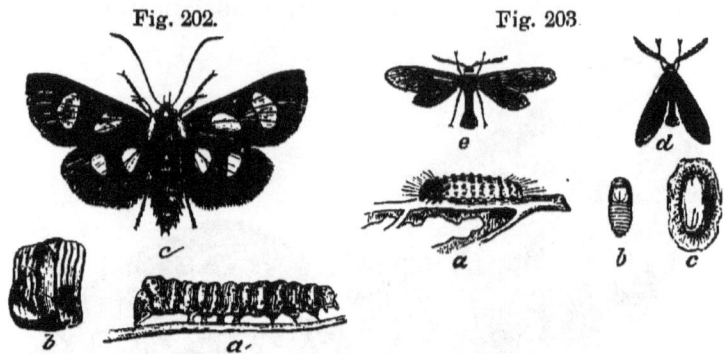

Fig. 202. Fig. 203.

SPINNERS (*Bombycidæ*).—These moths are nocturnal in their habits; the body is quite stout, the head is small and apparently sunken into the thorax, the antennæ are frequently

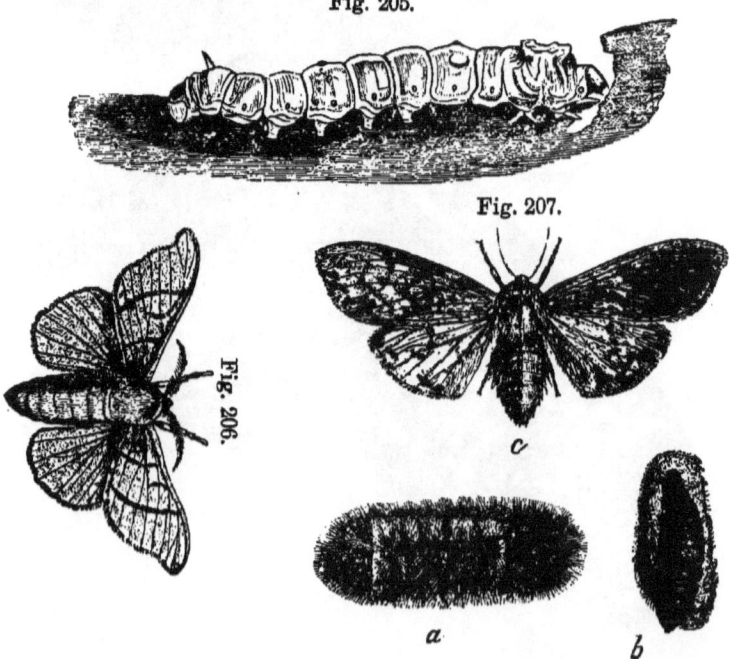

Fig. 205.

Fig. 206.

Fig. 207.

pectinated, the palpi are very short, and the wings are usually quite large, but the females of a few species are wingless.

Fig. 208.

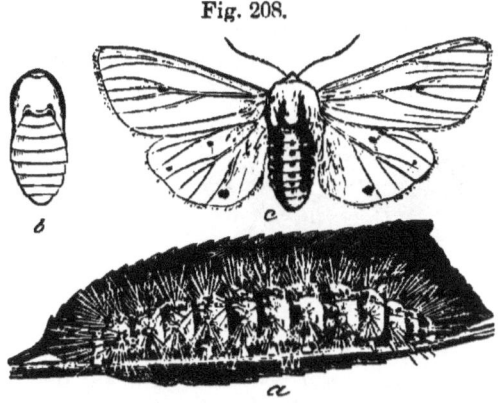

Their caterpillars are provided with sixteen legs, but in some these are very small, so that they appear to glide over the surface, like a slug; in others the last pair are imperfect.

Fig. 209.

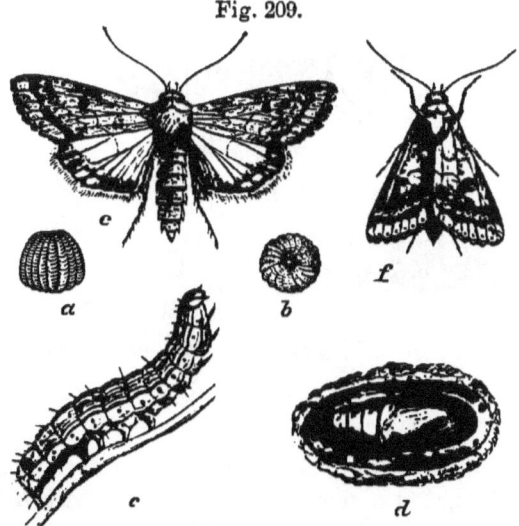

Some are naked, while others are clothed with hairs or spines. Some live exposed upon the leaves: others live beneath a web, or in a nest of leaves; a few construct cases in which to dwell, while a still smaller number live within the trunks of trees. The greater number spin cocoons in which to undergo their transformations. The Cecropia Moth and Caterpillar (Figs. 204 and 50); the Silk Worm and Moth (Figs. 205 and 206); the Isabella Moth (Fig. 207), and the White Miller (Fig. 208), are examples of this Family.

Fig. 210.

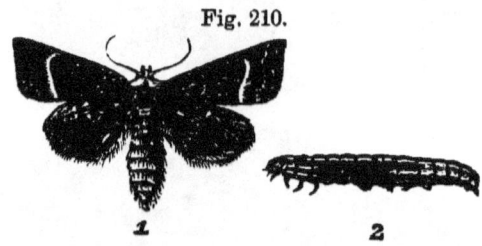

OWLET MOTHS (*Noctuidæ*).—These moths usually have the thorax or abdomen tufted; the head is not sunken into the thorax, the palpi are stout and well developed, the antennæ are usually simple, and the wings are quite large.

Fig. 211.

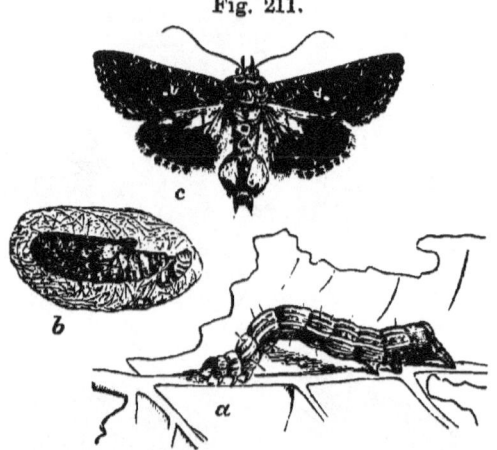

Their caterpillars have from twelve to sixteen legs, and are usually naked, but a few kinds are covered with hairs. The greater number live exposed upon the leaves, but a few kinds live within the stems of plants, in the ground, or in decayed wood. A few kinds spin cocoons, but the greater number enter the earth to pupate.

CLASSIFICATION OF INSECTS INTO FAMILIES. 71

The Corn Worm and Moth (Fig. 209); the Stalk Borer and Moth (Fig. 210); the Cabbage Plusia (Fig. 211); the Figure 8 Minor Moth and its caterpillar, the Bristly Cut Worm (Fig. 212), are examples of this Family.

Fig. 212.

GEOMETRID MOTHS (*Phalænidæ*).—These moths usually have long, slender bodies; the thorax is never tufted, the legs are long and slender, the anterior tibiæ are usually unarmed, and the hind tibiæ are usually armed with one or two pairs of spurs. The head is small and free, or not sunken into the

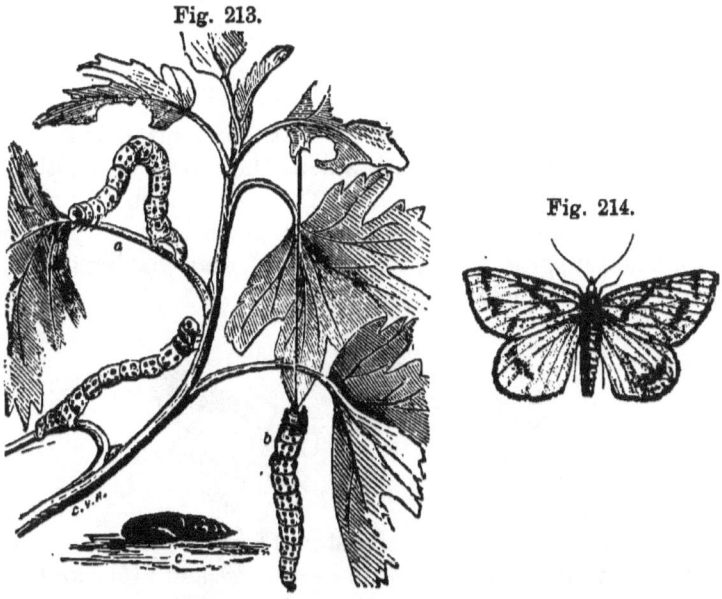

Fig. 213.

Fig. 214.

thorax, the antennæ are usually simple, but sometimes pectinate; the palpi are rather small and slender, the wings are usually triangular, broad and thin, and spread out in repose, and the stigmatæ* are wanting. In a few species the females are wingless.

The caterpillars live exposed upon the leaves; they are naked, and are provided with from ten to fourteen legs; in walking, they arch up the middle of the body and bring the hind feet close up to the front ones, thus seeming to span or measure the surface over which they pass, on which account they are commonly called "Span-worms," or "Measuring-worms." When disturbed, they usually drop from their perch and hang suspended by a silken thread, and when they think the danger is past, they climb up the thread to their former position. They frequently hold the body stretched out and attached only by the hind feet, and while in this position may easily be mistaken for small twigs.

Fig. 215.

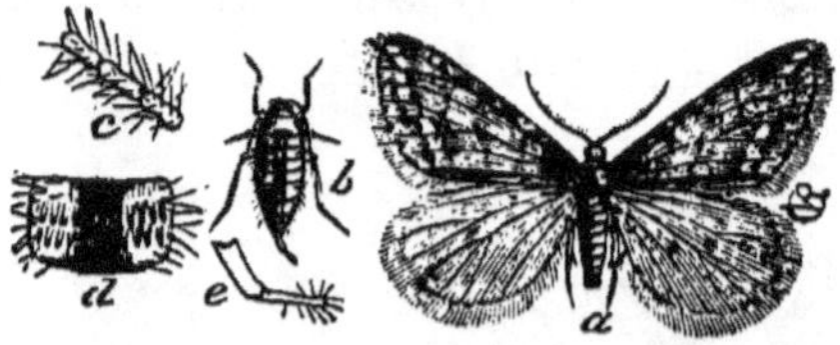

The greater number enter the earth to pupate, but some kinds spin their thin cocoons among the leaves, while others are said to suspend themselves. The specific names of those species the males of which have pectinate antennæ, usually terminates in *aria*, while the names of those having the antennæ simple commonly terminate in *ata*.

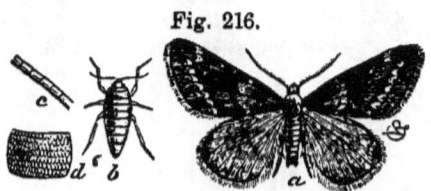

Fig. 216.

The Currant Span Worm and Moth (Figs. 213 and 214); the Spring Canker Worm and Moth (Figs. 150 and 215); and the Fall Canker Worm and Moth (Figs. 151 and 216), are examples of this Family.

---

* A term applied to the "orbicular" and "reniform" spots. (See Fig. 121.)

SNOUT MOTHS (*Pyralidæ*).—These moths have the body quite long and slender; the antennæ are not pectinate, the palpi are usually very long, and the legs are mostly unarmed.

Fig. 217.

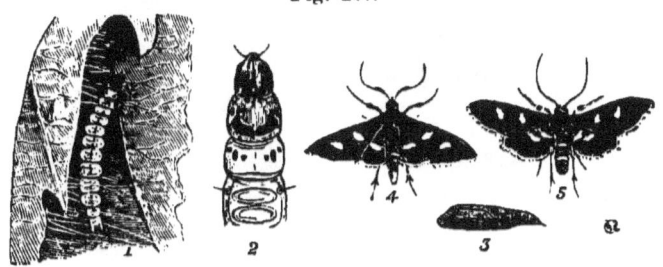

The caterpillars are naked, and are usually provided with sixteen legs. They generally live in silken tubes or cases, in a nest of leaves, or in fruit.

Fig. 218.

Fig. 219.

The Grape Leaf Folder (Fig. 217); the Clover Hay Worm (Fig. 218), and the Gooseberry Fruit Moth (Fig. 219) are examples of this Family.

LEAF-ROLLERS (*Tortricidæ*).—These moths are usually quite small; the antennæ are simple and short, the palpi are very short, and the fore-wings are nearly of the same width throughout, and are usually considerably rounded on the front edge.

The caterpillars are naked, and provided with sixteen legs; they live in a rolled leaf, or in a nest of leaves, and a few kinds live in fruit. The specific names of these insects usually terminate in *ana*.

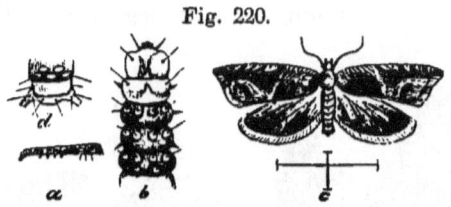

Fig. 220.

The Strawberry Leaf Roller (Fig. 220); the Cherry Leaf Roller (Fig. 221); the Bud Worm and Moth (Fig. 222), and the Codlin Moth (Fig. 223), are examples of this Family.

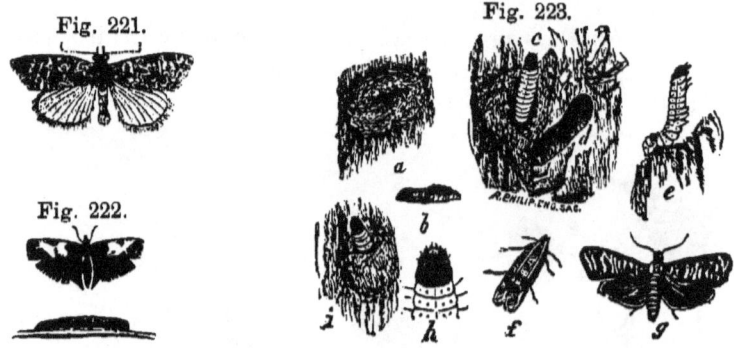

Fig. 221.

Fig. 223.

Fig. 222.

LEAF-MINERS (*Tineidæ*).—These moths are of small size; the body is slender, the wings are commonly pointed and heavily fringed, the palpi are usually long and curved in front of the head, and the antennæ are usually long and simple.

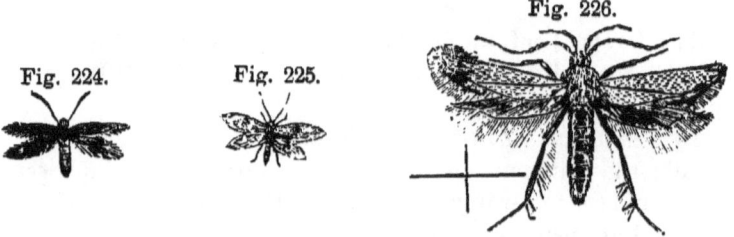

Fig. 224. Fig. 225. Fig. 226.

The caterpillars are naked, and usually provided with sixteen legs, but in very small species there is sometimes a greater number of legs than sixteen, while some are wholly destitute of legs. Some kinds live in a rolled leaf, others live in mines in the leaves, while still others live in carpets, woolens, furs, seeds, etc. The specific names of these moths usually terminate in *ella*.

The Potato Moth (Fig. 224); the Clothes Moth (Fig. 225), and the Grain Moth (Fig. 226), are examples of this Family.

PLUME MOTHS (*Pterophoridæ*).—These moths are mostly of a small size, and may easily be recognized by having the forewings once or twice notched or cleft, to or near the base, and the hind wings are twice cleft.

Fig. 227.

The caterpillars usually live exposed upon the leaves of plants; they are thinly covered with short, stiff hairs, and are provided with sixteen legs. When about to pupate they fasten themselves to some object by the under side of the hind part of the body. The chrysalids are usually angular and sparsely hairy.

The specific names of these insects usually end in *dactylus*.

The Grape Plume Moth (Fig. 227) is an example of this Family.

CHAPTER XIV.

ORDER III. DIPTERA. (*Two-winged Flies*).

The insects belonging to this Order are divided into two Sections, as follows :

SECTION I.—LONG-HORNED FLIES (*Nemocera*).—In these insects the antennæ are usually long and composed of four or more joints. None of these flies are beneficial, while several species are sometimes very injurious. The pupa has the members inclosed in separate sheaths.

SECTION II.—SHORT-HORNED FLIES (*Brachycera*).—In these insects the antennæ are short and from two to three jointed, although in a few kinds the last joint appears to be divided into two or more joints by impressed circles, but the difference between these circles and the true divisions is easily observed. These organs are sometimes bent down upon the face, and the last joint is frequently furnished with a short bristle (*arista*), which is sometimes pectinate or plumose. Some of these insects are beneficial, but the greater number are injurious. The pupa sometimes has the different members inclosed in separate sheaths, but in the greater number the pupa is inclosed in the hardened skin of the larva.

SECTION I. LONG-HORNED FLIES. (*Nemocera.*)

MOSQUITOES (*Culicidæ*).—In these insects the mouth parts consist of six slender pieces or lancets. The larvæ are aquatic and feed upon decaying vegetable matter. It is only the female mosquitoes that manifest the blood-thirsty propensity, the males being perfectly harmless (Fig. 228).

GALL-GNATS (*Cecidomyidæ*).—These insects are usually of small size; the wings are furnished with three or four longitudinal veins, and when at rest are usually laid flatly upon the back. The greater number of these insects live in galls, but a few kinds live in decayed vegetable matter, and one species, which is closely related to the Wheat Midge, feeds upon the gall-inhabiting form of the Grape Phylloxera. This Family contains the Hessian Fly (Fig. 18), Wheat Midge (Fig. 229), etc.

CRANE FLIES (*Tipulidæ*).—These insects are usually of a large size, and have very long, slender legs; the wings usually have a discal cell, the ocelli are generally wanting, the tibiæ are not beset with spines, although they are often spurred at the tip. In the genus *Chionea* the wings are wanting. The larvæ usually live in the ground and feed upon the roots of plants, but in a few species they are aquatic. (See Figs. 8 and 168.)

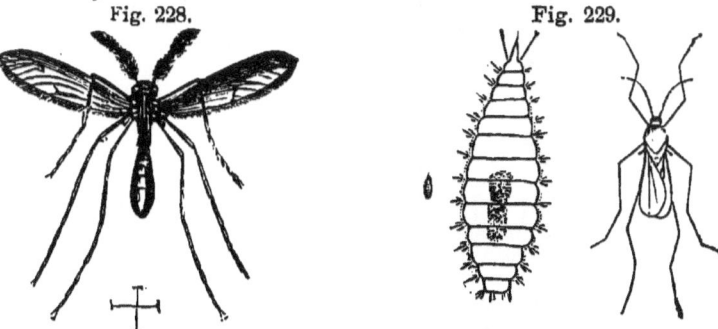

Fig. 228.   Fig. 229.

FLEAS (*Pulicidæ*).—These insects are destitute of wings, and the eyes are simple. This family contains the Fleas, etc. One species, the Chigoe, or Jigger, burrows beneath the skin of man and many animals.

SECTION II. SHORT-HORNED FLIES. (*Brachycera*.)

HORSE FLIES (*Tabanidæ*).—These insects have a perfect discal cell in their wings, the third longitudinal vein is forked, and the third joint of the antennæ is destitute of a style, or bristle. The larvæ are aquatic, or live in damp situations, and commonly feed upon snails, etc.; the pupæ are naked (*obtected*). The female flies subsist upon the blood of animals, while the males feed upon the nectar of flowers. The Black Horse Fly (Fig. 230) belongs to this Family.

SYRPHUS FLIES (*Syrphidæ*).—These flies have a perfect discal cell in each wing, the first posterior cell is closed, and there is usually a spurious or false vein extending part way through the first basal and first posterior cells. These insects fly very rapidly, and sometimes balance themselves on the wing, like a hawk; they are usually banded with yellow, somewhat like a wasp. They feed upon the nectar of flowers. The larvæ of a few species are aquatic, but the greater number are terrestrial and feed upon plant-lice; one species, however, the Nar-

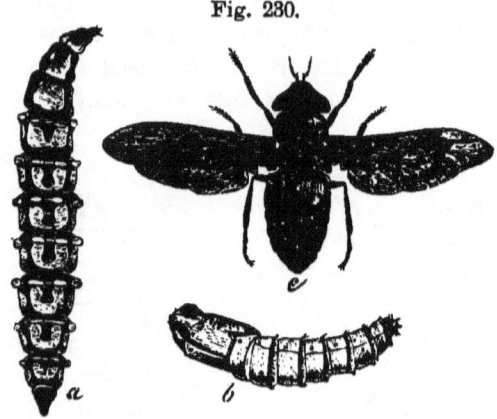

Fig. 230.

cissus Fly, is said to live in the soil, around decayed bulbs. The pupæ are coarctate, and the slender anterior end of the larva becomes the thickened end in the pupa. (See Figs. 231 and 232.)

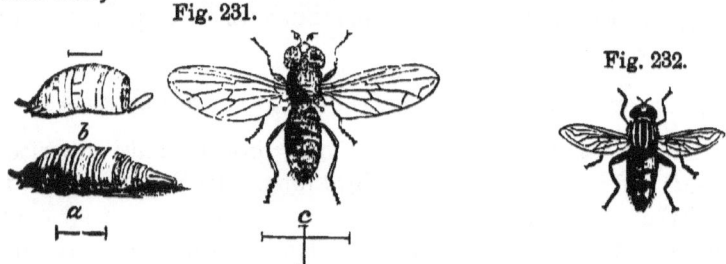

Fig. 231.   Fig. 232.

Bot Flies (*Œstridæ*).—These flies usually have very small antennæ, which are situated in rounded pits or depressions; the mouth parts are small, and often rudimentary; the body is stout and hairy, and the middle of the face is usually very narrow. The larvæ live in the bodies of various animals, and enter the earth to pupate; the pupæ are coarctate. The female flies are usually oviparous, but one species, the Sheep Bot Fly (Fig. 233), is stated by Prof. Riley to be viviparous. The Ox Bot Fly (Fig. 234) and the Horse Bot Fly (Fig. 235) belong to this Family.

HORSE FLIES (*Muscidæ*).—These flies have the third joint of the antennæ furnished with a style which is sometimes pectinate, or plumose, but is sometimes simple; the longitudinal veins of the wings are not forked, and the proboscis usually ends in a fleshy lobe. The pupæ are coarctate.

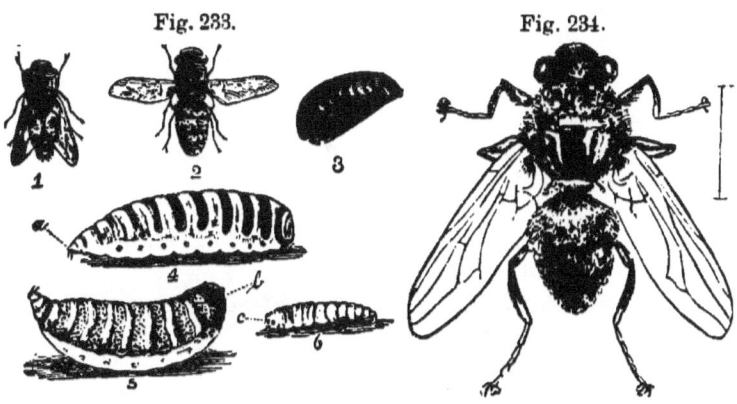

Fig. 233. Fig. 234.

In the Tachina Flies, the antennal style is simple, or not usually pectinate. These Flies (Fig. 236) are among the most beneficial of insects, since the larvæ live within the bodies of caterpillars, etc., ultimately causing their death.

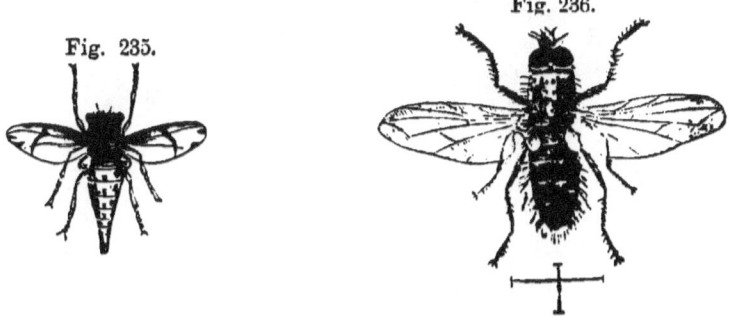

Fig. 235. Fig. 236.

Many kinds of flies have the antennal style either pectinate or plumose, such as the Blow Flies, Flesh Flies, House Flies, Stable Flies, etc. The larvæ live in various situations, such as in excrements, in decayed animal or vegetable matter, in galls on plants, or in the roots, stems or leaves of plants, in fruit, etc., and are hence to be regarded as mostly injurious.

One species, however, the *Anthomyia calopteni*, is eminently beneficial, as it feeds upon the eggs of those grasshoppers or locusts which deposit their eggs in the ground. The Flesh Flies (Fig. 23) bring forth their young alive. One of these flies has been bred from a wasp's nest which was filled with dead spiders.

CHAPTER XV.

Order IV. COLEOPTERA (*Beetles*).

The insects belonging to this Order are divided into four Sections, according to the number of joints* in their feet; these Sections are as follows:

Section I.—Beetles with five-jointed feet (*Pentamera*.) (See Fig. 103.)

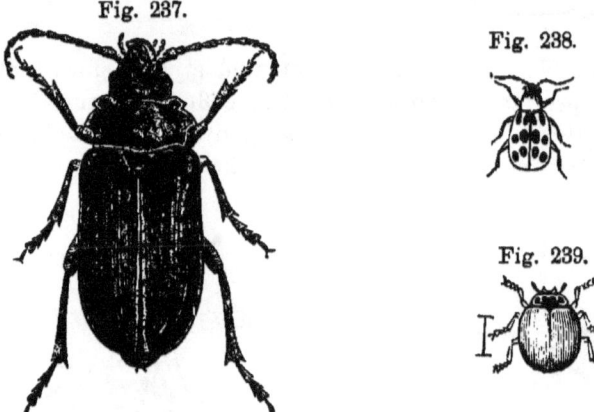

Fig. 237.

Fig. 238.

Fig. 239.

Section II.—Beetles with five joints in the anterior and middle feet, and only four joints in the posterior feet (*Heteromera*). (See Fig. 119.)

Section III.—Beetles with four joints in all the feet (*Tetramera*); such as the Broad-necked Prionus Beetle (Fig. 237), and the Twelve-spotted Diabrotica (Fig. 238).

---

*By the term "joint" is meant the *node* or part between two joints; in this sense the part of the arm between the joints of the elbow and wrist, would be called a *joint*. The joints of the foot (*tarsus*) are numbered from the shin (*tibia*) outwards; thus the joint next the shin is the first joint; the one next to this the second, etc.

CLASSIFICATION OF INSECTS INTO FAMILIES.

SECTION IV.—Beetles with only three-jointed feet (*Trimera*); such as the Trim Lady Bird (Fig. 239).

SECTION I. *PENTAMERA.*

A few small insects are placed in this Section, which apparently have a less number of joints in their feet than five; in these the first joint is aborted, or rudimentary; these species are included in the Sub-sections II and III, defined below.

The insects belonging to this Section may be divided into six Sub-sections, as follows:

SUB-SECTION I. (*Filicornes.*)—Antennæ thread-like (*filiform*), sometimes tapering to the tip (Fig. 94); habits predaceous.

SUB-SECTION II. (*Clavicornes.*)—Antennæ becoming thicker toward the tip (*clavate*, Fig. 92). These insects mostly feed upon decaying vegetable or animal matter.

SUB-SECTION III. (*Monilicornes.*)—Antennæ bead-like (*moniliform*); wing-cases very short. These insects usually feed upon decayed animal matter.

SUB-SECTION IV. (*Pecticornes.*)—Antennæ pectinate or comb-toothed (Fig. 102); they feed on decayed wood.

SUB-SECTION V. (*Lamellicornes.*)—Antennæ lamellate (Figs. 100 and 101). These insects feed upon excrements or on plants.

SUB-SECTION VI. (*Serricornes.*)—Antennæ usually saw-toothed (*serrate*, Fig. 99). Some of these insects are predaceous, but the greater number live within the stems or branches of shrubs or trees.

SUB-SECTION I. (*Filicornes.*)

The insects belonging to this Sub-section may be divided into two Tribes, as follows:

TRIBE I. Predaceous Ground Beetles.—These insects are mostly terrestrial in their habits, and usually prey upon other insects; the hind pair of trochanters are very large, much larger than in any other insects.

These Beetles are divided into two Families, as follows:

TIGER BEETLES (*Cicindelidæ*).—These insects have the head nearly vertical and wider than the thorax; the antennæ are inserted on the front, and the wing-cases are usually marked with white and yellow.

The larvæ are provided with six legs; they live in holes in the ground, and feed upon caterpillars and other insects.

Fig. 240.   Fig. 241.   Fig. 242.

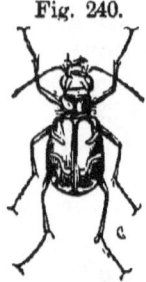

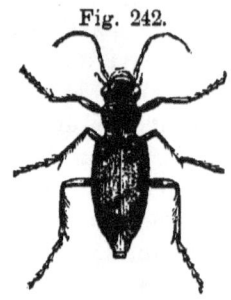

The Common Tiger Beetle (Fig. 240); the Generous Tiger Beetle (Fig. 241), and the Virginian Tiger Beetle (Fig. 242) are examples of this Family.

GROUND BEETLES (*Carabidæ*).—These insects have the head horizontal, or but little inclined, and usually narrower than the thorax; the antennæ are inserted under the sides of the front, and the color is mostly black.

Fig. 243.

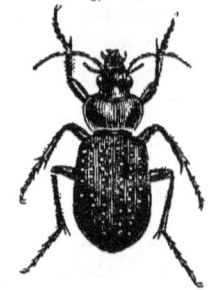

The larvæ are provided with six legs; they live in the ground, beneath logs, etc., and feed upon other insects. The adults are usually predaceous, but one or two species have been known to feed upon the green seeds of various plants. The Gold-spotted Ground Beetle (Fig. 243) is an example of this Family.

TRIBE II. Predaceous Water Beetles.—These insects are aquatic in their habits, and prey upon other insects. They comprise two Families, as follows:

DIVERS (*Dytiscidæ*).—In these insects the antennæ are slender and filiform, and the hind pair of legs are widely separated from the middle pair.

The larvæ are provided with six legs. The Margined Water Beetle (Fig. 244)* belongs to this Family.

---

* FIG. 244.—The larva (*a*) and the pupa (*b*) are not those of the beetle figured at *c*; *d* is the anterior foot of a male; *e*, that of a female.

WHIRLIGIG BEETLES (*Gyrinidæ*).—These Beetles have the third joint of the antennæ very large, and dilated on one side; the eyes are divided in the middle; the hind pair of legs are not further separated from the middle pair than the first pair are.

Fig. 244.

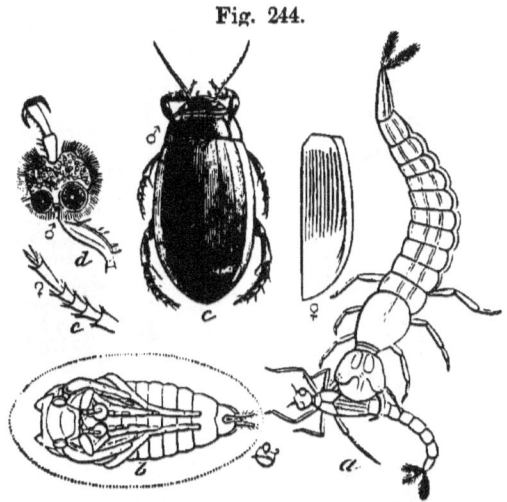

These insects are frequently seen swimming in circles upon the surface of the water. The larvæ are six-legged, and usually have a row of long appendages on each side of the body.

SUB-SECTION II. (*Clavicornes.*)

These insects may be divided into two Tribes, as follows:

TRIBE I. Water Scavenger Beetles.—These Beetles are aquatic in their habits, and usually feed upon decayed vegetable matter; they generally have the antennæ strongly clavate, and the palpi are sometimes longer than the antennæ. They belong to two Families, as follows:

LONG-TOED WATER BEETLES (*Parnidæ*).—These insects have the last joint of each foot very long, the feet sometimes are only four jointed, the palpi are moderate in length, and the legs are not fitted for swimming.

The larvæ are furnished with six legs, and the adults are usually found in moist or wet places.

SHORT-TOED WATER BEETLES (*Hydrophilidæ*).—In these Beetles the last joint of each foot is not much longer than the other joints; the palpi are very long, and the legs are usually fitted for swimming.

Fig. 245.

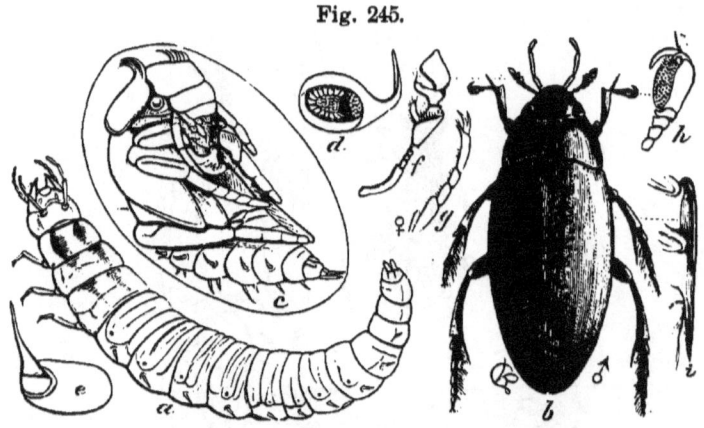

The larvæ of a few species are predaceous, but the greater number of them feed upon decomposing matter; they are provided with six legs. The Triangular Water Beetle (Fig. 245)* belongs to this Family.

Fig. 246.

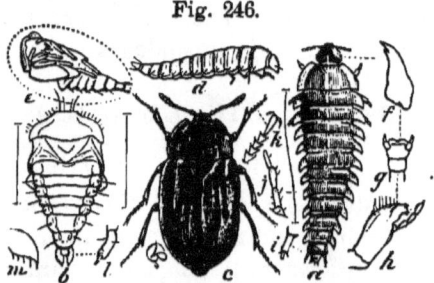

TRIBE II. Land Scavenger Beetles.—These insects are terrestrial in their habits, and feed upon decaying or dead animals, upon fungus, etc., and a few kinds are found beneath the bark of dead trees. They may be divided into two Sub-tribes, as follows:

---

* The larva (*a*) and pupa (*c*) are not those of the beetle figured at *b*; *e* is an egg case; *d*, the same cut open; *f*, an antenna; *g*, anterior foot of a female; *h*, same of a male; *i*, side view of the spine on the breast.

Sub-tribe I.—In these insects the body is rather broad, and the antennæ are clavate or capitate, with three or more pieces in the club. The principal Families are as follows:

Burying Beetles (*Silphidæ*).—These insects are mostly of a large size, usually over half an inch in length; the hind trochanters are large, and the thorax has a thin margin.

These Beetles feed upon dead animals, which, if not too large, they usually bury in the earth, to serve as food for their young. The latter are flattened, and provided with six legs. The Black Burying Beetle (Fig. 246)* belongs to this Family.

Museum Beetles (*Dermestidæ*).—These insects are less than half an inch long; the abdomen is covered by the wing-cases, and the breast is prolonged beneath the head.

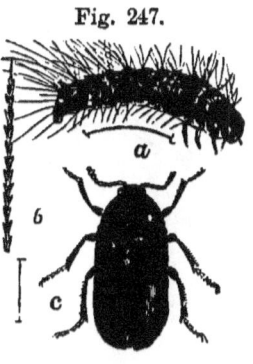

Fig. 247.

They feed upon dead animal matter (including insects), and several kinds are sometimes very destructive to carpets.

The larvæ are usually hairy and provided with six legs. The Raw-hide Beetle (Fig. 247) belongs to this Family. (It is sometimes called the Bacon Beetle, from its habit of feeding on bacon, ham, etc.)

Sub-tribe II.—In this division the body is more or less elongated; the antennæ are filiform or loosely clavate, sometimes with less than three pieces in the club.

The insects belonging to this Sub-tribe are mostly predaceous. The principal Families are as follows:

Trogosita Beetles (*Trogositidæ*).—These insects have all the feet five-jointed, but the first joint is sometimes very small, so that it cannot be seen from above; the colors are black or dull red; the club of the antenna consists of three joints, which are not conspicuously larger than the others; the last joint of each foot is very long.

These insects are usually found beneath the bark of trees, or in granaries, where they prey upon other insects. The larvæ are six-legged.

---

* Fig. 246. *a*, the larva; *f*, its upper jaw; *g*, its lower lip; *h*, its lower jaw; *j*, its antenna; *k*, anterior foot of the beetle.

Cucujus Beetles (*Cucujidæ*).—These insects have the feet apparently four-jointed; the body is flattened; the antennæ are usually moniliform, and the jaws usually project in a conspicuous manner in front of the head; the color is brown or red.

Fig. 248.

They are usually found under the bark of trees, but some kinds inhabit the granary, where they feed upon the grain, bran, etc. The larvæ are provided with six legs. The Bran Beetle (Fig. 248) belongs to this Family.

Sub-section III. (*Monilicornes*.)

These insects mostly belong to the Rove Beetle Family (*Staphylinidæ*); the wing-cases never cover more than one half of the abdomen (Fig. 249); the body is long and slightly flattened, and composed of eight segments; the jaws usually cross each other when at rest.

Fig. 249.

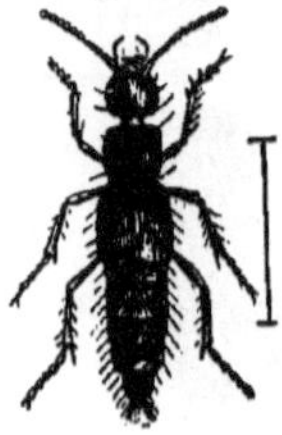

These Beetles usually turn up their long flexible abdomens when running, and they use this in folding up their wings beneath the wing-cases.

The greater number feed upon decaying animal and vegetable matter, but some are predaceous; others live in the nests of ants; while one species has been bred from the pupa of a Cabbage Maggot.

The larvæ (Fig. 172) are provided with six legs.

Sub-section IV. (*Pecticornes*.)

This Sub-section includes the single Family of Stag Beetles (*Lucanidæ*), in which the antennæ are usually elbowed (*geniculate*); the joints of the club are immovable, and the jaws of the males are greatly developed.

These insects are usually of a large size, seldom measuring less than half an inch in length; they feed upon the sap exuding from trees.

The larvæ live in decaying wood; their bodies are usually curved when at rest, and they are provided with from four to six legs.

SUB-SECTION V. (*Lamellicornes.*)*

In these insects the joints in the club of the antennæ are immovable. This Sub-section includes two Tribes of widely separate habits; these are as follows:

TRIBE I.—These insects usually have the abdomen entirely covered by the wing-cases, and the hind legs are attached behind the middle of the abdomen.

These Beetles live in excrementitious matter, or in decomposing animal matter. They are commonly called "Tumble Bugs," and comprise the Families *Copridæ, Aphodidæ, Geotrupidæ* and *Trogidæ.*

TRIBE II.—In this Tribe the tip of the abdomen is never covered by the wing-cases, and the hind pair of legs are placed at or before the middle of the abdomen.

These Beetles feed upon fruits or the leaves of plants, and their larvæ live in the ground and usually feed upon the roots of plants. The three principal Families are as follows:

JUNE BEETLES (*Melolonthidæ.*)—In these insects the thorax is unarmed; the upper lip is usually visible in front of the clypeus; the latter is separated from the front by a transverse suture; the two claws at the end of each foot are forked; and the color is usually brown, sometimes striped with white.

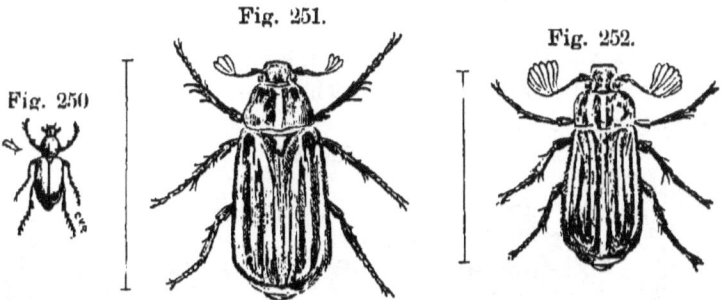

Fig. 250. Fig. 251. Fig. 252.

This Family includes the destructive White Grub (*Lachnosterna quercina,* Fig. 139, 2), and many other insects which, in the larva state, feed upon the roots of plants, while the adults feed upon the leaves.

---

* The insects belonging to this Sub-section are sometimes included in one Family—the *Scarabæidæ.*

The larvæ have the body curved, and furnished with six legs. The Rose Chafer (Fig. 250), the Ten-lined Leaf Eater (Fig. 251, female; Fig. 252, male), belong to this Family.

GRAPE-VINE BEETLES (*Rutelidæ*).—These insects closely resemble those of the preceding Family, but the claws at the end of each foot are of an unequal length; all of the claws are not forked, and the colors are brown or blackish.

Fig. 253.

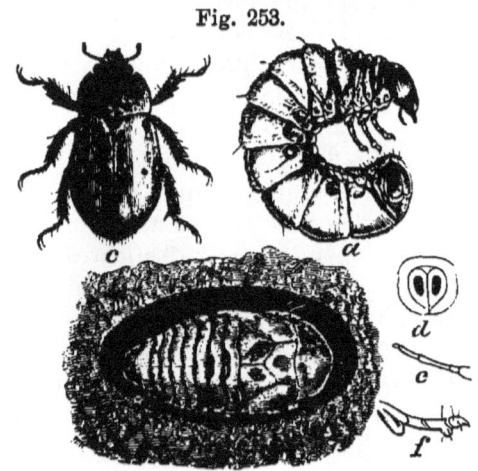

These insects are sometimes very destructive to the leaves of various trees, and especially to those of the grape-vine. The larvæ are similar to those of the preceding Family, and usually live in decayed wood. The Spotted Pelidnota (Fig. 253) belongs to this Family.

Fig. 254. Fig. 255.

CETONIANS (*Cetonidæ*).—These insects usually have the wing-cases flattened above, and slightly narrower at the tip than at the base; the two claws at the end of each foot are of

CLASSIFICATION OF INSECTS INTO FAMILIES.   89

the same length, and are not forked, and the clypeus is not separated from the front by a transverse suture.

Many of these insects are diurnal in their habits, and do not raise the wing-cases when flying; they feed upon the fruit or leaves of plants, and, in the larval stage (Fig. 255, *a*), a few species live in decayed wood. The Indian Cetonia (Fig. 254) and the Green Fruit Beetle (Fig. 255) belong to this Family.

SUB-SECTION VI. (*Serricornes.*)

The insects which belong to this Sub-section are divided into three Tribes, as follows:

TRIBE I. Saw-horned Borers.—In these Beetles the head is inserted into the thorax up to the eyes; the wing-cases are

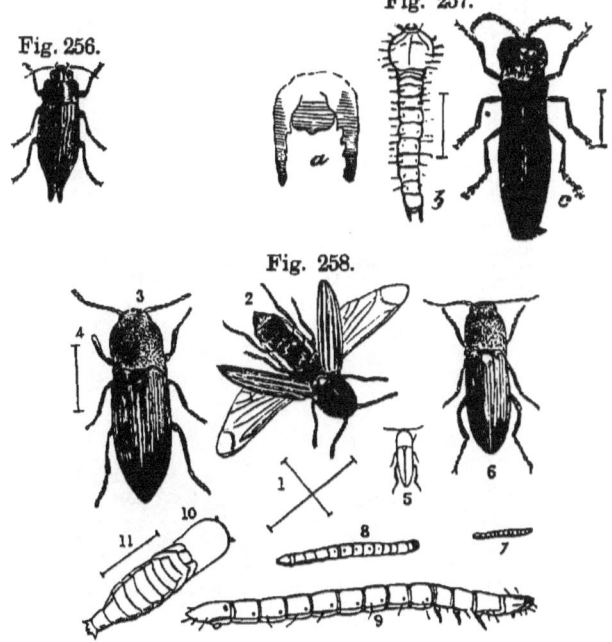

Fig. 256.

Fig. 257.

Fig. 258.

of a hard, firm texture; the antennæ are sometimes filiform, and the breast is prolonged behind into a point, which is received in a cavity in the next segment. These insects comprise two Families, as follows:

90 NATURAL HISTORY OF INSECTS.

BUPRESTIS BEETLES (*Buprestidæ*).—In these insects the point at the hind part of the breast is immovable; the antennæ are finely serrate, and the colors are usually metallic.

The larvæ usually have the fore part of the body greatly dilated and flattened (Fig. 54,), and the body is nearly or wholly destitute of legs; they live in the stems, roots or trunks of plants, shrubs or trees, and are sometimes very destructive. One of these, the Flat-headed Apple-tree Borer (Fig. 138), is very destructive to various kinds of fruit trees. The Cherry-tree Borer (Fig. 256) and the Raspberry Borer (Fig. 257) belong to this Family.

Fig. 259.

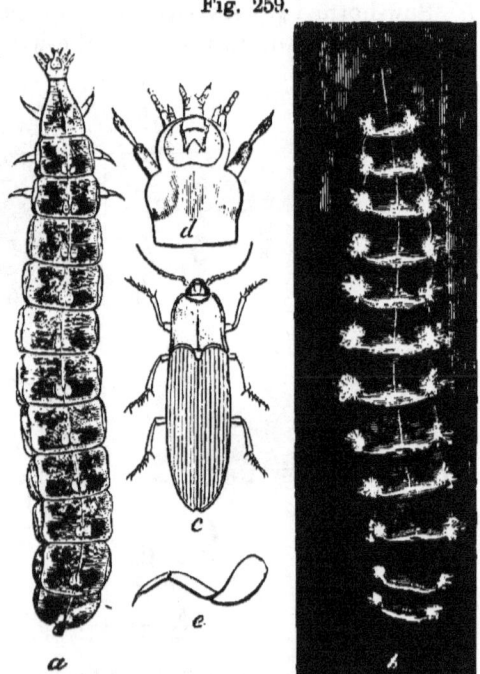

SPRING BEETLES (*Elateridæ*).—In these insects the point at the hind end of the breast is movable; the antennæ are sometimes filiform, and the colors are usually brown or black.

They are at once distinguished from all other insects by

the power they possess of suddenly springing into the air when placed on their backs upon any hard, smooth surface.

The larvæ live in decayed wood or in the ground, and are provided with six or seven legs, and are commonly known as "Wire-worms" (Fig. 258, 7, 8 and 9); some kinds feed upon the roots of various plants, but a few species are partially predaceous. The Skip-jack Beetles (Fig. 258, 2, 3 and 6,) and the Black Melanactus (Fig. 259)* belong to this Family.

TRIBE II. Aberrant Wood Beetles.—These insects usually have the head bent down and partially or wholly concealed beneath the thorax, which is frequently prolonged in front; in some the body is elongated, the head is free and exposed, and the first segment is very long.

These insects live in wood, both in decayed wood and in that which is solid, and a few species feed upon dead animals and are injurious to cabinets of Natural History. The following is the principal Family:

Branch Borers (*Ptinidæ*).—These insects have the fore part of the thorax produced like a hood, partially or wholly concealing the head when viewed from above; the first segment of the abdomen is very long; there is sometimes only four joints in the feet, and the color is usually black or brown.

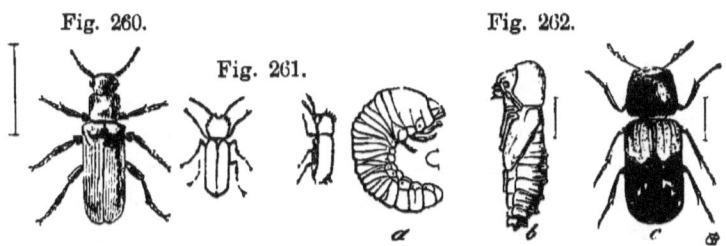

Fig. 260. Fig. 261. Fig. 262.

The larvæ have the body curved, and furnished with six legs. The Branch and Twig Burrower (Fig. 260), the Branch Borer (Fig. 261), and the Red-shouldered Grape-vine Borer (Fig. 262) belong to this Family.

TRIBE III. Soft-winged Beetles.—These insects usually have soft bodies and thin flexible wing-cases; the antennæ are

---

* The larva figured at *a* and *b* are supposed to belong to this species, and appears after night as a Glow-worm, showing a beautiful green light.

generally serrate; the terminal joint of the palpi is widened and somewhat triangular; the thorax is usually surrounded by a thin margin; and the fourth joint of each foot is bilobed.

These insects are predaceous, both in the larva and in the perfect state; the larvæ usually have the body nearly straight and provided with six legs. The following is the principal Family:

LIGHTNING BEETLES (*Lampyridæ*, also called "Fire-flies").—In these Beetles the body is rather soft, and the thorax has a thin margin which sometimes projects over the head; the abdomen has seven or eight segments; the color is usually black or brown, and some kinds have the thorax margined with red or yellow. Many of these Beetles possess a luminous power, both as larva and as perfect insects. The Common Fire-fly (Fig. 263) belongs to this Family.

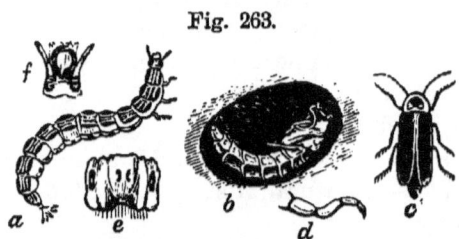

Fig. 263.

SECTION II. *HETEROMERA*.

The insects belonging to this Section are very uniform in having only four joints in the posterior feet; as a whole they are not eminently injurious. They may be divided into three Tribes, as follows:

TRIBE I. Parasitic Beetles.—In these insects the head is as wide as the thorax, and attached to it by a visible neck; the body is rather soft, the wing-cases flexible and the anterior coxæ meet each other (are contiguous). The two principal Families are as follows:

BLISTER BEETLES (*Meloidæ*).—These insects have the thorax rounded at the sides; the abdomen is not distinctly pointed behind; and the claws at the end of each foot is forked.

The larvæ are usually provided with six legs, and live in the nests of Bees, or in the egg-masses of such Grasshoppers or Locusts as deposit their eggs in the ground; the perfect insects feed upon the leaves or flowers of plants.

The insects belonging to the genus, *Meloe*, are destitute of hind wings.

Several species belonging to the genera *Lytta*, *Cantharis*, *Epicauta*, etc., possesses a blistering (*vesicating*) property, and to this group belongs the common Spanish Fly. The Striped Blister Beetle (Fig. 19) and the Ash-colored Blister Beetle (Fig. 86) belong to this Family.

NOTOXUS BEETLES (*Anthicidæ*).—These are small insects, a little over two lines long, with filiform antennæ; the claws are not forked; the thorax is sometimes prolonged in the form of a horn (Fig. 264), which projects over the head; the neck is usually slender, and the head can be moved to either side from under the extension of the thorax. These beetles have been known to feed on flowers, and have been found eating into peaches, apricots, etc.

Fig. 264.

TRIBE II. Bark Beetles.—In these insects the fore coxæ nearly or quite touch each other; the head is narrower than the thorax, and the antennæ are usually quite long and slender. The larvæ live in decayed wood. The two principal Families are the *Cistelidæ* and the *Melandryidæ*.

TRIBE III. Ground Beetles.—In these insects the anterior coxæ do not touch each other, there are five joints in the abdomen, the antennæ are usually moniliform, and the color is generally black or brown.

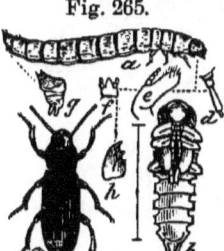

Fig. 265.

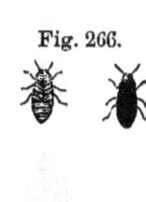

Fig. 266.

The larvæ are more or less cylindrical, and provided with six legs; they closely resemble the larvæ of the Spring-beetles, commonly called "Wire-worms;" the greater number live in decayed wood, but some kinds, such as the Meal Worm (Fig. 265, *a*,) are found in granaries, flour mills, etc.

They are all included in the Family of Darkling Beetles (*Tenebrionidæ*). The Large Darkling Grape Beetles (Fig. 119), the Meal Worm Beetle (Fig. 265, *c*), and the Small Darkling Grape Beetle (Fig. 266), belong to this Family.

SECTION III. *TETREMERA.*

In this Section the joints of the feet are usually dilated and brush-like, and the next to the last joint is usually bilobed; there is occasionally in some small species a rudimentary joint between the third and fourth joints.

This Section contains a greater number of injurious insects than all the other Sections combined. They are divided into four Tribes, as follows:

TRIBE I.—These insects have the head more or less prolonged into a snout; the antennæ are usually capitate, sometimes clavate or serrate, and frequently elbowed.

The two principal Families are as follows:

Fig. 267.

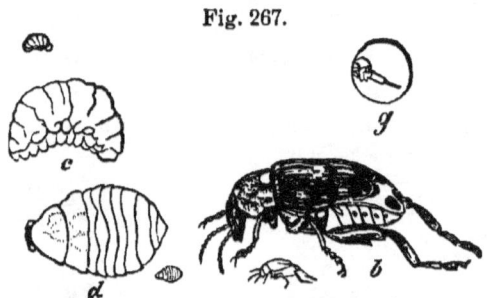

BRUCHUS WEEVILS (*Bruchidæ*).—In these insects the snout is short and thick, the antennæ are serrate and not elbowed, and the eyes are notched.

Fig. 268.

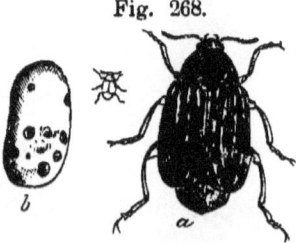

These insects are of small size, and the wing-cases do not cover the tip of the abdomen.

The larvæ are footless, and usually live in seeds. To this Family belong the well known Pea-weevil (Fig. 267), and the Bean Weevil (Fig. 268).

SNOUT BEETLES (*Curculionidæ*).—These Beetles are destitute of an upper lip and palpi; the antennæ are clavate and usually elbowed; the snout generally projects downward, and is sometimes very long and slender.

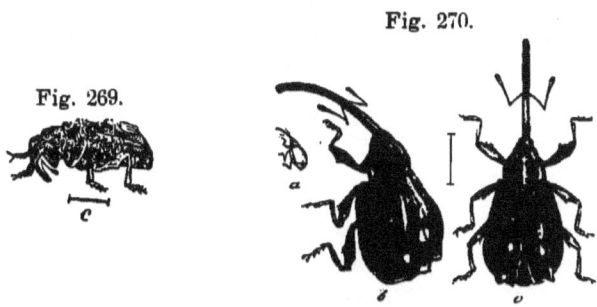

Fig. 269.   Fig. 270.

The larvæ are footless, and are provided with a distinct head; they live in fruits, nuts, seeds, etc.; in fact, there is scarcely a single part of a plant that is not sometimes infested by them.

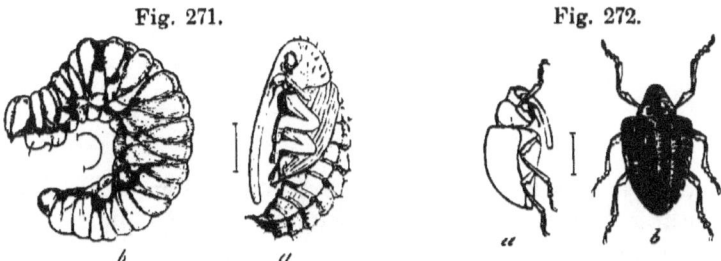

Fig. 271.   Fig. 272.

In depositing her eggs, the female first gnaws a hole with her jaws, which are placed at the tip of her snout, then deposits her egg at the entrance of this hole, after which she turns around and, with her snout, pushes the egg to the bottom of the hole. The Plum Curculio (Fig. 269), the Apple Curculio (Figs. 270 and 271), the Quince Curculio (Fig. 272), the Plum Gouger (Fig. 273), the Potato-stalk Weevil (Fig.

274), and the Strawberry Crown Borer (Fig. 275), belong to this Family.

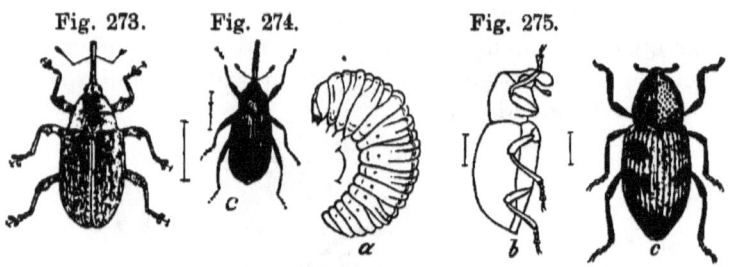

Fig. 273. Fig. 274. Fig. 275.

TRIBE II. Short-horned Borers.—In these the head is not prolonged into a snout; the body is usually short and cylindrical; the antennæ are clavate or capitate, and but little longer than the head; and the joints of the feet are not dilated.

These insects are of small size, and usually of a black or brown color. The larvæ bore winding galleries in the solid wood and are frequently very destructive, especially to forest trees. These insects belong to the Family of Short-horned

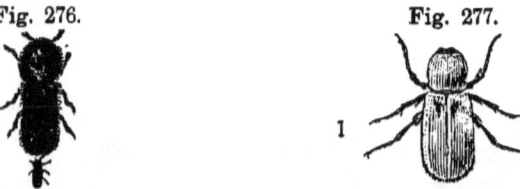

Fig. 276. Fig. 277.

Borers (*Scolytidæ*). The Pear-tree Scolytus (Fig. 276) and the Chestnut Bud Beetle (Fig. 277) belong to this Family.

TRIBE III. Long-horned Borers.—In these insects the body is elongated and the antennæ are long and tapering, usually longer than the thorax, and frequently as long as the entire body; the males usually have longer antennæ than the females. The sides of the thorax are generally furnished with spines or teeth.

A few of these Beetles have very short wing-cases, like the Rove Beetles, but the wings are not folded up and concealed beneath the wing-cases, as they are in the latter insects.

The larvæ (Fig. 278, *a*,) are footless, or nearly so, and live in the stems or branches of various plants, shrubs or trees, while a few live in decayed wood.

Fig. 278.

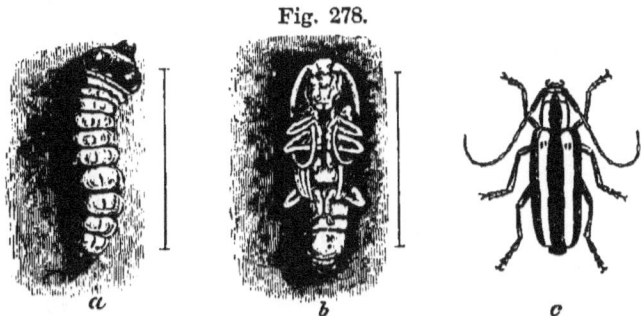

These insects belong to the Family of Long-horned Borers (*Cerambycidæ*), and are among the most destructive of insects. Hidden as they are from the eyes of man, they carry on their silent work of destruction unnoticed, until the withering plant apprises us of the presence of these destructive depredators.

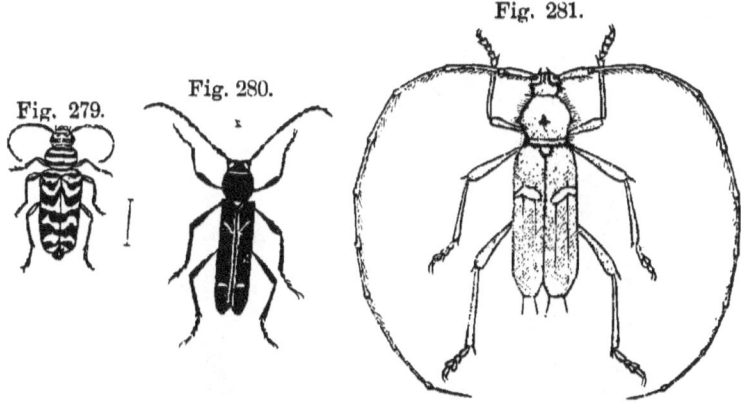

The Round-headed Apple-tree Borer (Fig. 278, *c*), the Hickory Borer (Fig. 281), the American Currant Borer (Fig. 280), and the Locust-tree Borer (Fig. 279) are examples of this Family.

TRIBE IV. Plant Beetles.—These are mostly small Beetles, seldom exceeding half an inch in length; the antennæ are either filiform or slightly clavate.

98   NATURAL HISTORY OF INSECTS.

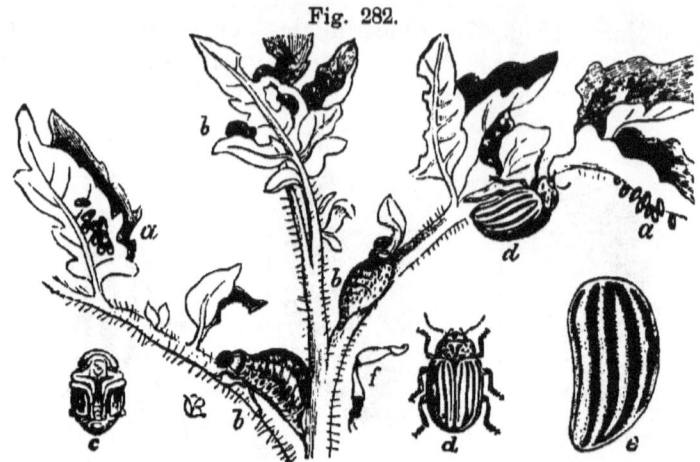

Fig. 282.

They are usually diurnal in their habits. The larvæ live upon or within the leaves or roots of plants; they are provided with six legs, and the body is usually short and convex.

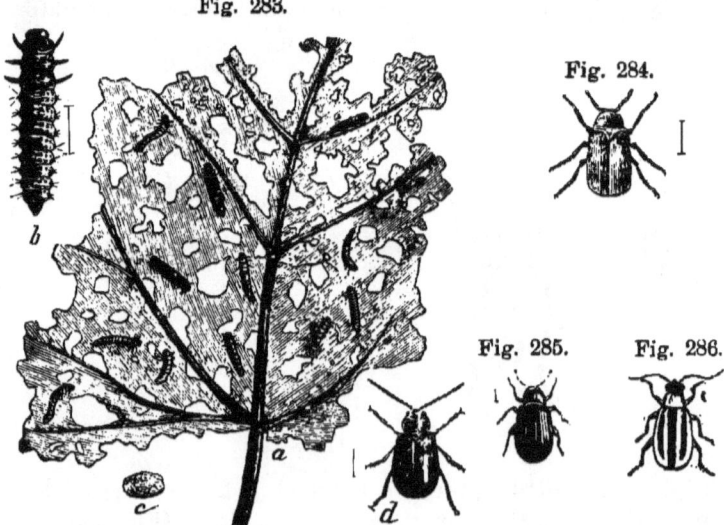

Fig. 283.   Fig. 284.   Fig. 285.   Fig. 286.

These insects are all destructive to vegetation; they belong to the Family of Plant Beetles (*Chrysomelidæ*). The Colorado Potato Beetle (Fig. 282), the Steel-blue Flea-beetle (Fig. 283), the Imported Grape Flea-beetle (Fig. 284), the Cucumber and Potato Flea-beetles (Fig. 285), the Striped Cucumber Beetle

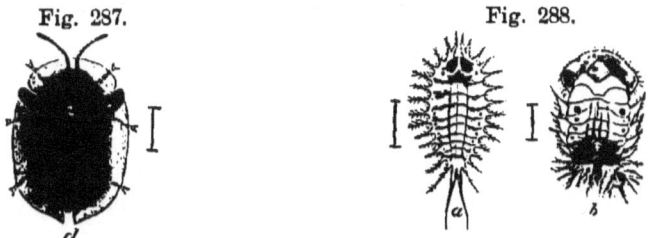

Fig. 287.   Fig. 288.

(Fig. 286), the Twelve-spotted Diabrotica (Fig. 238), and the Tortoise Beetles (Figs. 287 and 288), belong to this Family.

SECTION IV. *TRIMERA*.

These insects are usually of a small size and more or less hemispherical in form; the last joint of the palpi is broadly hatchet-shaped; the joints of the feet are dilated and cushion-like beneath, and the second joint is deeply bilobed.

These insects belong to the Lady-bird Family (*Coccinellidæ*), and their colors are usually red or black, never, or very seldom, marked with stripes. They all prey upon Plant-lice, Scale Insects, small caterpillars, etc., although in a very few instances, they have been known to attack fruit (as the California Lady-bird, Fig. 289), but this habit is very exceptional.

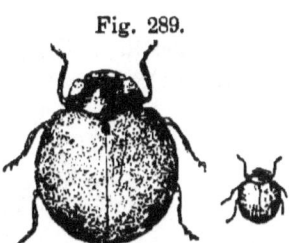

Fig. 289.

The larvæ are furnished with six legs, and when about to pupate they attach themselves to some object by the hind part

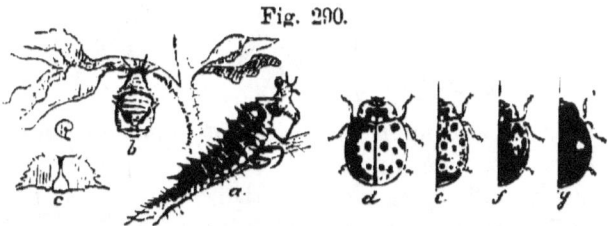

Fig. 290.

of the body. The Fifteen-spotted Lady-bird (Fig. 290) is a good representative of this Family.

CHAPTER XVI.

ORDER V. HEMIPTERA. (*True Bugs.*)

SUB-ORDER I. HOMOPTERA. (*Similar-winged Bugs.*)

PLANT-LICE (*Aphididæ*).—These insects are usually provided with four transparent wings, but many of them are wingless; the feet are two-jointed; the antennæ are from three to seven jointed, and are never terminated by two

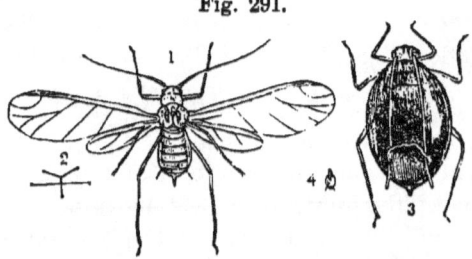

Fig. 291.

bristles; the abdomen is usually provided with two tubercles, or long tubes, near the posterior end, and the beak appears to arise from the breast. These insect are usually of a small

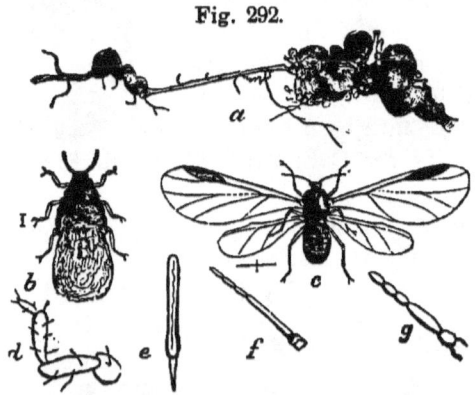

Fig. 292.

size; they subsist upon the juices of plants, and are found upon the roots, stems and leaves, and a few species form galls. They are usually gregarious in their habits, and the early broods of many species are viviparous, while the last broods of the season are oviparous.

From their honey-tubes they occasionally eject a sweet fluid, of which the ants and flies are very fond. The Cabbage Aphis (Fig. 24), the Grain Aphis (Fig. 291), and the Woolly Aphis (Fig. 292) belong to this Family.

MEALY-WINGED BUGS (*Aleurodidæ*).—These insects have four opaque wings, which are covered with a mealy powder;

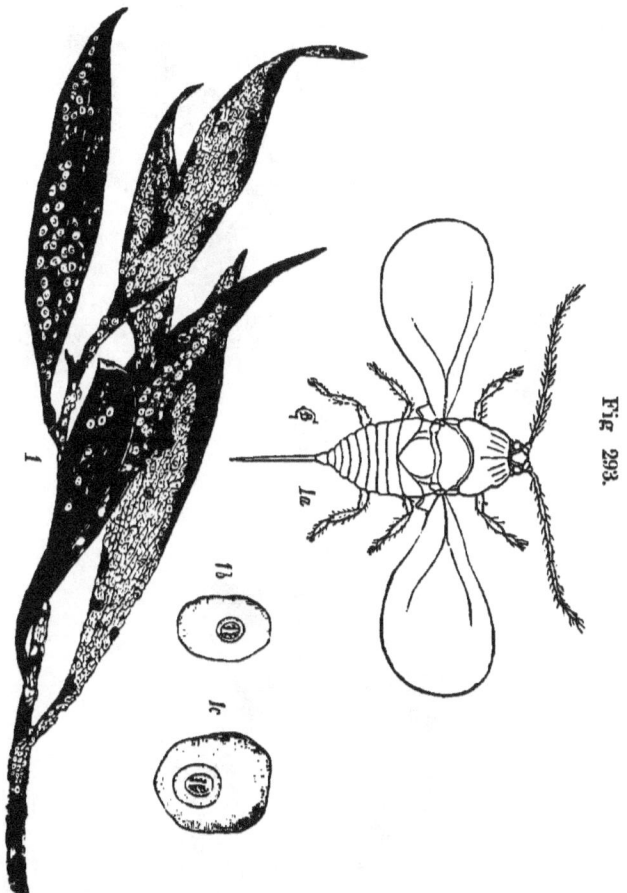

Fig. 293.

the feet are two-jointed, and the beak apparently arises from the breast; the antennæ are six-jointed. These insects are of small size, and feed upon the juices of plants.

SCALE INSECTS (*Coccidæ*).—In these insects, which are

Fig. 294.

Fig. 295.

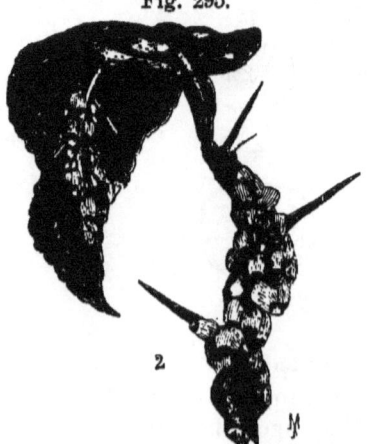

sometimes called "Bark-lice," the females (Fig. 293, $1c$,) are wingless, while the males (Fig. 293, $1a$,) are each provided with two more or less transparent wings; the feet are one-jointed and terminate in a single claw. Some species are oviparous, while others are viviparous. The Lemon-peel Scale (Fig. 293), the Black Scale (Fig. 294), and the Cottony Cushion Scale (Fig. 295) belong to this Family. [For additional examples see Chapter on Scale Insects.]

JUMPING PLANT-LICE (*Psyllidæ*).—The insects belonging to this Family are of small size, and have four transparent wings; the feet are two jointed; the antennæ are nine or ten jointed, the last joint terminating in two short bristles; the beak

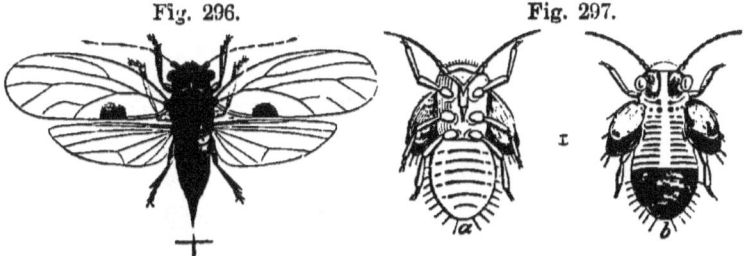

Fig. 296.   Fig. 297.

apparently arises from the breast. These insects possess the power of jumping; they subsist upon the juices of plants, and a few species live in galls. The Pear-tree Psylla (Fig. 296, *adult;* 297, *pupæ*,) belongs to this Family.

LEAF-HOPPERS (*Cercopidæ*).—These insects are provided with four wings, the first pair of which are thick and leathery;

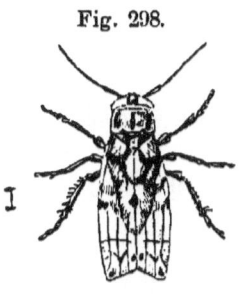

Fig. 298.

the feet are three-jointed; the ocelli are only two in number, or are entirely wanting; and the antennæ are two-jointed. In a few species the thorax arises in the form of a hump or a horn, or like a high crest; in others it is produced each side in the form of a small horn (as in the Buffalo Tree-hopper, Fig. 155). These insects subsist upon the juices of plants, and a few kinds envelope themselves in a mass of froth called "frog-spittle." The California Grape-vine Hopper (Fig. 298) belongs to this Family.

LANTERN FLIES (*Fulgoridæ*).—These insects are provided with four wings, the first pair of which are usually opaque; the feet and antennæ are three-jointed, and the head is sometimes furnished with a high, thin ridge; the two ocelli are placed beneath the eyes. The Frosted Leaf-hopper (Fig. 299) belongs to this Family.

Fig. 299.

HARVEST FLIES (*Cicadidæ*).—These insects, improperly termed "Locusts," are provided with four large transparent wings; the feet are three-jointed; the antennæ small, and six or seven jointed, and on the top of the head are three ocelli. These insects are of a large size; they deposit their eggs in slits made in the twigs of trees (Fig. 300, *d*), and the young,

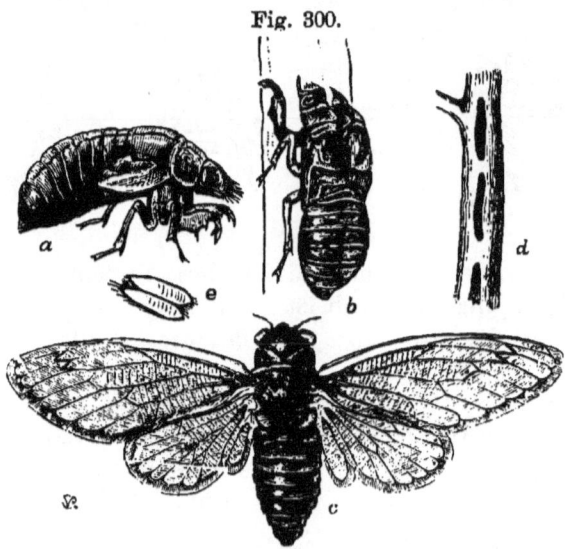

Fig. 300.

when hatched, drop to the ground, which they enter and are supposed to feed upon the roots of plants. One species, the Seventeen-year Locust (Fig. 300), requires seventeen years to complete its growth.

CHAPTER XVII.

ORDER V. HEMIPTERA. (*True Bugs.*)

SUB-ORDER II. HETEROPTERA (*Dissimilar-winged Bugs.*)

WATER BOATMEN (*Notonectidæ*).—These insects have convex bodies and are provided with four wings; the hind legs are very long and fringed; the antennæ are minute and concealed in cavities; the feet are two or three jointed; the ocelli are wanting, and the head is nearly as wide as the body.

These insects reside in the water and are predaceous in their habits; they seldom exceed six lines in length.

WATER SCORPIONS (*Nepidæ*).—These insects have very flat bodies and are furnished with four wings; the anterior legs are fitted for grasping, and are placed well forward; the antennæ are minute and are concealed in cavities; the feet are one or two jointed, and the ocelli are wanting.

These insects are aquatic, and feed upon other insects; they are usually of quite a large size.

GALGULA BUGS (*Galgulidæ*).—In this Family the body is broad and flat and provided with four wings; the antennæ are minute and concealed in cavities; the eyes are placed at the outer end of a stem or pedicel; the ocelli are present; the feet are one or two jointed, and the anterior thighs are enlarged.

These insects live in damp situations, and are supposed to feed upon other insects; they are usually smaller, although of nearly the same form, as the enlarged figure in Fig. 304.

WATER MEASURERS (*Hydrometridæ*).—These insects have a long slender body, and are usually provided with four wings, but in a few species these organs are wanting; the antennæ are quite long and slender; the ocelli are sometimes wanting; the feet are two or three jointed, and the four posterior legs are usually very long and slender.

These insects are aquatic, and the adults may frequently be seen running over the surface of the water; they feed upon other insects and are usually less than six lines long.

PIRATE BUGS (*Reduridæ*).—In this Family the body is usually elongated and provided with four wings, but in a few species these are either rudimentary or entirely wanting; the antennæ are conspicuous; the ocelli are present; the feet are three jointed; and the beak when folded back is not received in a channel.

A few species are aquatic, but the greater number are terrestrial and feed upon other insects. The Banded Robber (Fig. 154) belongs to this Family.

CHINCH BUGS (*Lygæidæ*).—These insects are provided with four wings; the antennæ are conspicuous and four-jointed, the terminal joint being as thick as the preceding one; the ocelli are sometimes absent.

These insects are terrestrial and usually subsist upon the juices of plants, but a few species are said to be predaceous. The Chinch Bug (Fig. 85) is sometimes very destructive to wheat and corn; it is of a black color with white wings which

Fig. 301.

are marked with a black spot on the outer edge of each. The False Chinch Bug (Fig. 301) also belongs to this Family.

SQUASH BUGS (*Coreidæ*).—These insects are furnished with four wings; the antennæ are conspicuous and four jointed, the terminal joint being as thick or thicker than the preceding one; the ocelli are present.

These insects are terrestrial and usually subsist upon the juices of plants, but a few species are said to be partially predaceous. The Squash Bug (Fig. 163) is sometimes very destructive to squash and pumpkin vines; it is blackish-brown above and dirty yellowish beneath, and measures about seven lines in length. The Three-striped Plant-bug (Fig. 302) also belongs to this Family.

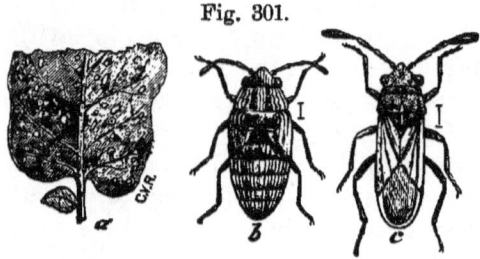

Fig. 302.

PLANT BUGS (*Capsidæ*).—These insects are terrestrial and are provided with four wings; the ocelli are absent; the antennæ are four jointed, with the terminal joint thinner than the preceding one.

Fig. 303.

These insects mostly subsist upon the juices of plants, but a few species are predaceous. The Bordered Plant-bug (Fig. 303) belongs to this Family.

SOLDIER BUGS (*Scutelleridæ*).—These insects usually have a broad and flattened body, and are furnished with four wings; the scutellum extends to or beyond the middle of the abdomen; the antennæ are conspicuous and are from three to five jointed.

Fig. 304.

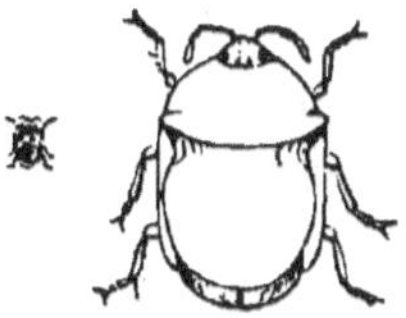

The greater number of these insects feed upon the juices of plants, but a few species feed upon other insects. The Spined Soldier Bug (Fig. 114) and the Negro Bug (Fig. 304) belong to this Family.

THRIPS (*Thripidæ*).—These insects are of a small size, and are provided with four narrow wings, which are fringed; the mouth is furnished with jaws; the ocelli are present; and the antennæ are from five to nine jointed.

Fig. 305.

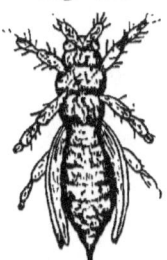

Some of these insects are vegetable feeders, while others are said to prey upon other insects. The Common Thrips (Fig. 161, *adult;* Fig. 305, *pupa,*) belongs to this Family.

BED BUGS (*Membranaceidæ*).—In this Family the body is quite broad, and is sometimes provided with four wings, but these organs are frequently wanting; the beak is received in a channel when not in use; the ocelli are usually wanting, the antennæ are usually four jointed, with the terminal joint thicker than the preceding one; the feet are three jointed.

Some of these insects subsist upon the juices of plants; others are predaceous; while a few, like the Bed Bug, are parasitic. The Tingis (Figs. 306 and 307, enlarged) belongs to this Family; it subsists upon the juices of plants.

Fig. 306.

Fig. 307.

LICE (*Pediculidæ*).—These insects are of a small size and are destitute of wings; the antennæ are filiform and five jointed; the feet are two jointed, with a large terminal hook; and the mouth parts are retractile.

These insects, so far as at present known, all live parasitically upon man.

BIRD LICE (*Mallophagidæ*).—These insects are of a small size and are destitute of wings; the mouth is furnished with jaws; the antennæ are from three to five jointed; the feet are two jointed, and usually terminate in one or two claws.

These insects live parasitically upon birds and animals.

CHAPTER XVIII.

ORDER VI. ORTHOPTERA. (*Grasshoppers, Crickets, etc.*)

This Order is usually divided into four Sections, as follows:

I. RUNNERS (*Cursoria*).—In this Section the body is not greatly elongated, and the legs are fitted for running.

II. GRASPERS (*Raptoria*).—The insects which belong to this Section have the anterior legs very robust and fitted for seizing and retaining their prey, which consists of other insects.

III. WALKERS (*Ambulatoria*).—These insects have long

cylindrical bodies, which are destitute of wings;* the legs are very long and slender, and the insects are very sluggish in their habits.

IV. JUMPERS (*Saltatoria*).—These insects have the posterior thighs very robust; they usually move by short jumps or leaps; the greater number are provided with four wings, but a few species are destitute of these organs.

I. RUNNERS (*Cursoria*).

This Section contains two Families, as follows:

EARWIGS (*Forficularidæ*).—These insects have a more or less cylindrical body, which is furnished at the tip with a forceps-like appendage; the wing-cases are very short, and meet each other in a straight line on the back; the hind wings when not in use are folded both lengthwise and crosswise, and concealed beneath the wing-cases.

These insects (Fig. 41) feed upon various kinds of fruits and flowers; they deposit their eggs beneath stones, etc., and in a few species the female broods over them, like a hen, until they are hatched.

COCKROACHES (*Blattidæ*).—The insects which belong to this Family have a flattened body, which is destitute of the anal forceps that characterizes the insects belonging to the preceding Family. In some species both sexes are wingless in the adult state; in others the males are provided with wings, while the females have these organs greatly aborted; and in still others, both sexes are furnished with wings.

These insects are nocturnal in their habits, and are sometimes very troublesome about the kitchen, etc. The female deposits her eggs in a large elongated brown capsule or pod, each capsule containing about thirty eggs, arranged in two rows.

II. GRASPERS (*Raptoria*).

This Section is composed of the Mantis Family (*Mantidæ*, Fig. 142); they are the only insects belonging to this Order which are beneficial. They deposit their eggs in masses of a

---

* Winged species occur in some tropical countries.

hundred or more (Fig. 308), fastening them to the twigs of trees or to other objects.

Fig. 308.

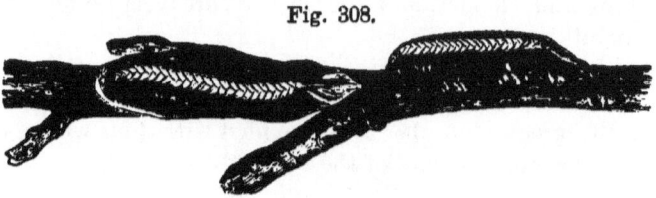

III. WALKERS (*Ambulatoria*).

This Section includes the single Family of Walking-sticks (*Phasmidæ*). These insects feed upon the leaves of plants, and sometimes occur in destructive numbers. The females scatter their eggs indiscriminately upon the ground beneath them.

IV. JUMPERS (*Saltatoria*).

This Section comprises three Families, as follows:

CRICKETS (*Gryllidæ*).—These insects have a more or less cylindrical body, and the anterior or upper wings are bent downward suddenly at the sides, although in a few species the wings are entirely wanting.

The Mole Crickets have the anterior pair of legs very robust and flattened at the outer end; they are provided with wings, and live in burrows in moist ground. The eggs are laid in large cavities excavated in their burrows.

The Tree Crickets (Fig. 309) are of a pale greenish color;

Fig. 309.

they are very slightly built, and are found upon various kinds of plants. The females deposit their eggs in slits made in some tender plant by means of their awl-like ovipositors. The males produce a shrilling noise by elevating their anterior wings and rubbing the edges together.

The Field Crickets are mostly of a brownish color, and many of them are entirely destitute of wings; they deposit their eggs in crevices in the earth.

KATYDIDS, OR GREEN GRASSHOPPERS (*Locustidæ*).—These insects (Fig. 141) are usually of a green color; their legs and antennæ are very long and slender, and the females are furnished with a sword-shaped ovipositor. The eggs are deposited in one or more rows upon the leaves or twigs of trees or plants (Fig. 310). The males make a shrilling noise by means of a glassy instrument, situated at the base of the anterior wings.

Fig. 310.

LOCUSTS, OR BROWN GRASSHOPPERS (*Acrididæ*).—These insects have shorter and stouter legs and antennæ than those belonging to the two preceding Families. They are mostly of a brownish color, and deposit their eggs in masses in holes excavated in the earth (Fig. 39), or in logs; these holes are excavated by the aid of the horny plates which are situated at the tip of the abdomen.

The males of a few species make a stridulating noise by rubbing their hind legs against the edges of the wing-covers; others produce a rattling sound, when on the wing, by rubbing the upper surface of the wings against the wing-cases.

These insects may be further divided into two Sub-families, as follows:

GROUSE LOCUSTS (*Tettiginæ*).—This group contains insects of a small size, in which the upper part of the thorax is prolonged backward nearly to the tip of the abdomen, and sometimes beyond it.

TRUE LOCUSTS (*Acridinæ*).—In this group the upper part of the thorax extends but little, or not at all, upon the base of the abdomen (Fig. 89). This group contains the more prominent injurious species, such as those which migrate in vast flocks or swarms.

CHAPTER XIX.

ORDER VII. NEUROPTERA. (*Dragon Flies, May Flies, etc.*)

WHITE ANTS (*Termitidæ*).—These insects are provided with four wings of equal size; the antennæ are conspicuous, and the feet are four jointed; transformations incomplete. The common White Ant is of a yellowish-white color, and is sometimes injurious to growing trees by gnawing the bark near the roots, but is more often met with in decayed wood.

FUNGUS FLIES (*Psocidæ*).—These insects are usually provided with four wings (Fig. 144), of which the hind pair is the smallest; in some, however, all the wings are rudimentary, while in others these organs are entirely wanting; the feet are from two to three jointed; and the antennæ are conspicuous; transformations incomplete. These insects usually feed upon dry vegetable substance, especially upon lichens, and a few kinds are injurious to collections of Natural History.

PERLA FLIES (*Perlidæ*).—These insects have four wings of equal size, or the hind wings are the broadest; all the wings are sometimes rudimentary; the antennæ are very long, and the feet are three jointed; in many species there are two long bristles at the posterior end of the abdomen; transformations incomplete. The larvæ of the greater number of these insects are aquatic.

MAY FLIES (*Ephemeridæ*).—The insects belonging to this Family usually have four wings, but the posterior pair are sometimes wanting; the mouth parts are obsolete; the antennæ are short and three jointed, and the abdomen is usually furnished at the tip with two or three slender bristles; the feet have from four to five joints; transformations incomplete. After issuing from the pupa the insect is usually enveloped in a thin film; it is now known as the *sub-imago;* it soon casts off this filmy covering and appears in the perfect (*imago*) state. The larvæ are aquatic, and feed upon other insects, etc.; they are supposed to remain from two to three years in the larva state, although the adults live but a few hours. These flies quite closely resemble the Ichneumon Flies (Fig. 131), but their antennæ are much shorter, and their bodies weaker.

DRAGON FLIES (*Libellulidæ;* also called *Odonata*).—These insects are provided with four wings of nearly equal size (Fig. 143); the antennæ are inconspicuous, and from four to seven jointed; the feet are three jointed, and the abdomen is destitute of anal bristles; transformations incomplete. The larvæ are aquatic, and feed upon other insects; they have a peculiar syringe-like apparatus, beneath the posterior part of the body, by which they are enabled to draw in a small quantity of water and then to forcibly eject it backward, thus propelling them forward at a rapid rate.

These insects are divided into two groups, viz:

Agrioninæ, in which the head is very broad; the eyes wide apart; and the wings, when at rest, are raised over the back.

Libellulinæ, in which the head is nearly globular; the eyes usually touch each other; and the wings are expanded when at rest (Fig. 143).

SIALIS FLIES (*Sialidæ*).—These insects are provided with four wings of nearly equal size; the antennæ are conspicuous, and the feet are four or five jointed; transformations complete. The larvæ are predaceous; some are aquatic, while others live upon trees, etc. In some species the pupa is capable of moving about, although enveloped in a thin covering or skin.

LACE-WINGED FLIES (*Hemerobidæ*).—The insects belonging to this Family have four wings of nearly equal size; the antennæ are long, and the feet are five jointed; transformations complete. The larvæ are usually terrestrial. This Family contains many beneficial insects; prominent among which are the Lace-winged (Fig. 22) and the Golden-eyed Flies, the larvæ of which (Fig. 47) feed upon Plant-lice; when full grown each of these larvæ spins a globular cocoon, inside of which it assumes the pupa form; when the perfect insect is nearly ready to emerge, the pupa issues from the cocoon and fastens itself to a neighboring object by its feet; in a short time the skin on its back is rent, and the perfect insect makes its escape. Another member of this Family is the Ant-lion, the larvæ of which excavate funnel-shaped holes in the earth in which to entrap their prey, which consists principally of Ants.

SCORPION FLIES (*Panorpidæ*).—These insects are usually provided with four wings of equal size, but in a few species the wings are rudimentary or wanting; the antennæ are conspicuous, and the feet are five jointed; transformations complete; the mouth parts are produced somewhat in the form of a beak. The larvæ are usually terrestrial, and are probably predaceous.

CADDIS FLIES (*Phryganidæ*).—These insects have four wings, in which the transverse veins are very few; the antennæ are quite long, and the feet are five jointed; the mouth parts are not distinct; transformations complete. The larvæ are usually aquatic. living in silken tubes, to which they frequently attach small shells, pieces of wood, and other small objects. They feed upon vegetable matter, and sometimes devour small insects.

CHAPTER XX.

Scale Insects.

The Scale Insects, Scale-bugs, Bark-lice, Mealy Bugs, etc., comprise a group of insects belonging to the Sub-order *Homoptera*, and to the Family *Coccidæ*.

In many respects this is a very anomalous group of insects, differing greatly even from closely allied forms, in appearance, habits and metamorphosis. Not only do the members of this Family appear very different from other insects belonging to the same Sub-order, but there is a wonderful variety of forms within the Family; and even the two sexes of the same species, in the adult state, differ as much in appearance as insects belonging to different Orders.

The most obvious characters in which these insects agree, and by which they may be distinguished from other insects belonging to the same Sub-order, are the following: The females never possess wings; the males are winged in the adult state, but possess only one pair of wings, the second pair being represented by a pair of small club-like organs called "halteres," each usually furnished with a bristle. The scale of the female is usually broader than that of the male in the scale-bearing species. This Family is divided into three Sub-families, as follows:

SUB-FAMILY I. (*Diaspinæ*.)—These insects are enclosed or covered by a scale composed in part of the moulted skins (*exuriæ*) and partly of an excretion of the insect; this scale does not adhere to any part of the insect's body, but forms a covering or protection to the latter.

SUB-FAMILY II. (*Lecaninæ.*)—These insects are not usually enclosed in a scale, but the skin hardens as the insect approaches maturity. In the earlier part of their lives these insects are capable of crawling about, but when nearly mature they generally become immovably fixed to the bark. etc., upon which they rest.

SUB-FAMILY III. (*Coccinæ.*)—These insects usually retain the power of locomotion from the time they are hatched until they die of old age or some other cause; some species, however, are destitute of legs, and are enclosed in a felt-like sac.

SUB-FAMILY I. (*Diaspinæ.*)

The following table will serve to aid in ascertaining the Genus to which any species of this Sub-family belongs:

A.—Scale of female circular, with the exuviæ either central or near the margin.
  B.—Scale of male but little elongated, with the exuviæ more or less central; scale usually resembling that of the female in color and texture. - - - *Aspidiotus*.
  BB.—Scale of male elongated, with the exuviæ at one extremity.
    C.—Scale of male, white and carinated - - *Diaspis*.
    CC.—Scale of male not white, and with no central carina. *Parlatoria*.
AA.—Scale of the female elongated, with the exuviæ at one extremity.
  D.—Exuviæ small.
    E.—Scale of male, white and carinated. - *Chionaspis*.
    EE.—Scale of male similar in form to that of the female. *Mytilaspis*.
  DD.—Exuviæ large.
    F.—Scale of female, with two moulted skins visible. *Parlatoria*.
    FF.—Scale of female with second moulted skin covered by a secretion. - - - - - - *Uhleria*.

Genus Aspidiotus (Bouche).

This genus includes species in which the scale of the female is circular, or nearly so, with the exuviæ at or near the center; and the scale of the male is somewhat elongated, with the larval skin at one side of the center, or near one extremity; in color and texture it resembles the female scale. The last

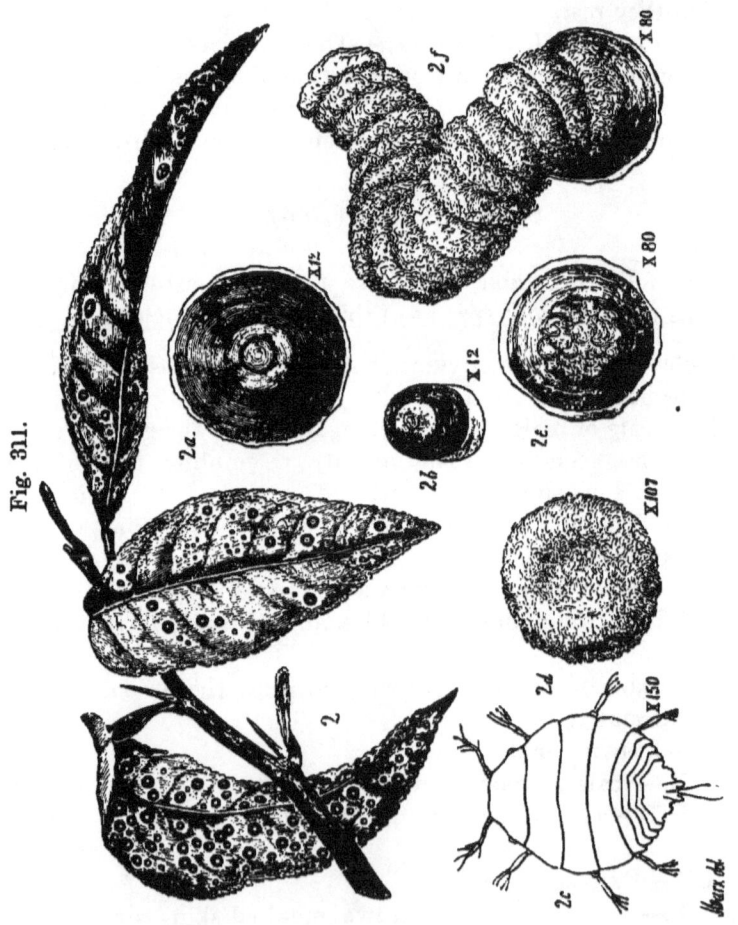

Fig. 311.

segment of the female usually presents four groups of spinnerets; in a few species there are five or six groups, and in some they are wanting. Examples—the Red Scale (Fig. 159), the

Lemon-peel Scale (Fig. 293), and the Red Scale of Florida (Fig. 311).

Genus DIASPIS (Costa).

This genus includes species in which the scale of the female is more or less rounded, with the exuviæ at the center or upon the sides; the scale of the male is long, white, carinated, and with the exuviæ at one extremity. The last segment of the female presents five groups of spinnerets.

Fig. 312.

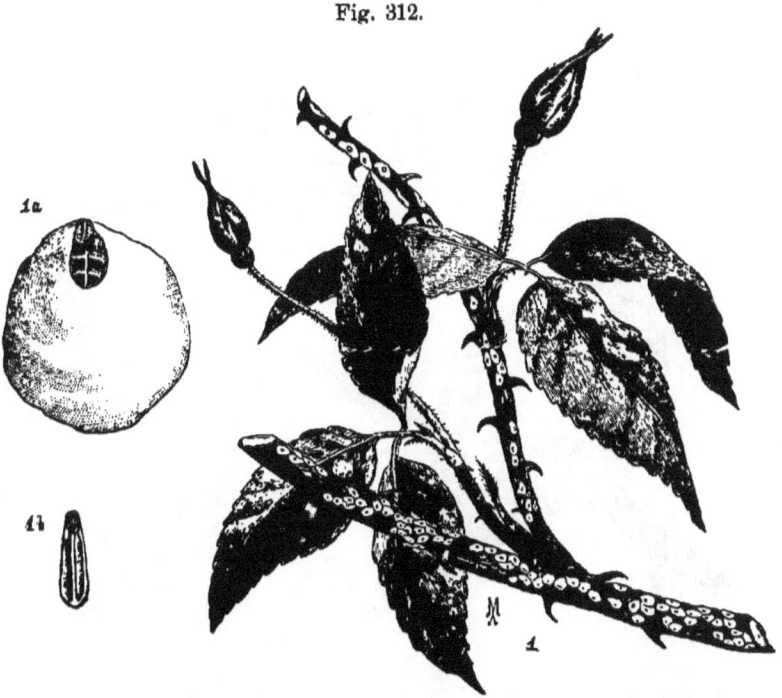

This genus closely resembles *Aspidiotus* in the form of the scale of the female, but it is easily distinguished from that genus by the scale of the male being white and carinated. Example—the Rose Scale (Fig. 312).

Genus CHIONASPIS (Signoret).

This genus includes species in which the scale of the female is long, sometimes much widened, with the exuviæ small and at one extremity; the scale of the male is long, generally white, more or less carinated (except in *C. ortholobis*), with the sides parallel and the larval skin at the anterior end. The last segment of the female presents five groups of spinnerets.

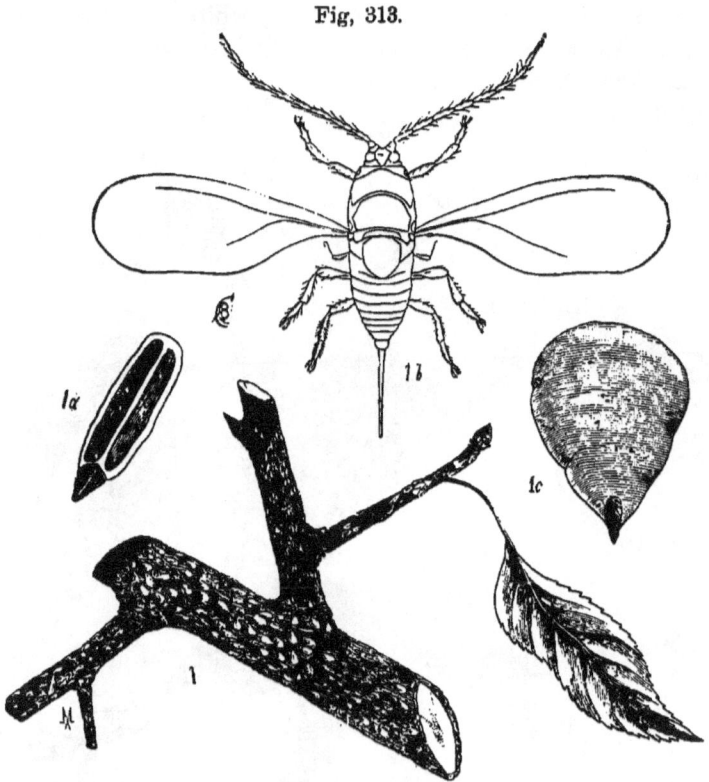

Fig, 313.

This genus resembles *Diaspis* in the form of the scale of the male, and *Mytilaspis* in the form of the scale of the female; in most species, however, the scale of the female is wider than in *Mytilaspis*. Example—the Scurfy or Harris' Scale (Fig. 313).

Genus MYTILASPIS (Targioni—Tozzetti).

This genus includes species in which the scale of the female is long, narrow, more or less curved, and with the exuviæ at the anterior extremity. The scale of the male resembles that of the female in form, but it can be readily distinguished by its small size, and by bearing but one larval skin. In all the species of *Mytilaspis* which I have studied, the posterior part

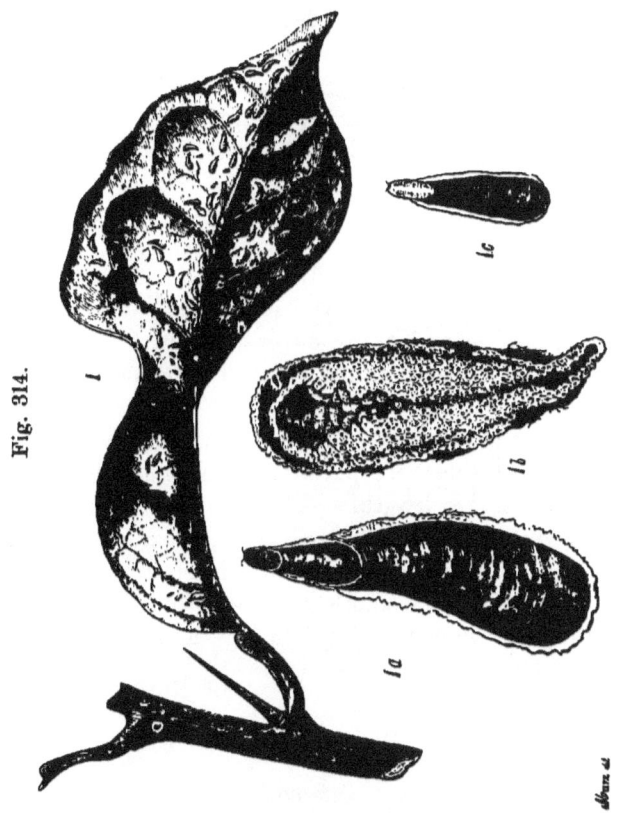

Fig. 314.

(about one fourth) of the scale of the male is joined to the remainder by a thin portion, which serves as a hinge, allowing the posterior part to be lifted when the male emerges. Example—the Citrus Scale (Fig. 314).

Genus PARLATORIA (Targioni—Tozzetti).

The scale of the female is either circular or elongated, with

the exuviæ large and at the anterior end. The scale of the male is elongated, with the sides nearly parallel and the exuviæ at the anterior end; there is no carina on the middle of the back, this part being seldom higher than the sides.

Fig. 315.

The margin of the last segment of the female is crenulated and fringed with toothed scale-like plates; there are only four groups of spinnerets. Example—Pergande's Orange Scale (Fig. 315).

Genus UHLERIA (Comstock).

This genus includes species in which, upon the scale of the female, only one larval skin is visible at the anterior extremity; the second skin is present, but it is entirely covered by secretion. This skin is large, covering the insect entirely.

Fig. 316.

The scale is narrow at its anterior end; it soon widens, and the sides are parallel throughout the greater part of its length. The three anterior groups of spinnerets are united, forming a continuous line. The scale of the male is similar to that of the female, but smaller. A small and unimportant genus, formerly known as *Fiorinia*. Example—the Camellia Scale (Fig. 316).

SUB-FAMILY II. (*Lecaninæ.*)

Genus CEROPLASTES.

The species belonging to this genus are furnished with a thick covering of waxy material, which does not, however, adhere closely to the insect. This covering is formed of layers secreted by the spinnerets. Some of the species have tuberosities upon the back which are larger or smaller, according to the age of the insect, and which entirely disappear at full growth, when, from being more or less flat with tuberosities, they become smooth and globular. The antennæ are six-jointed, the third being the longest. In the larva state the fourth and fifth appear as one. The legs are long; the claw is

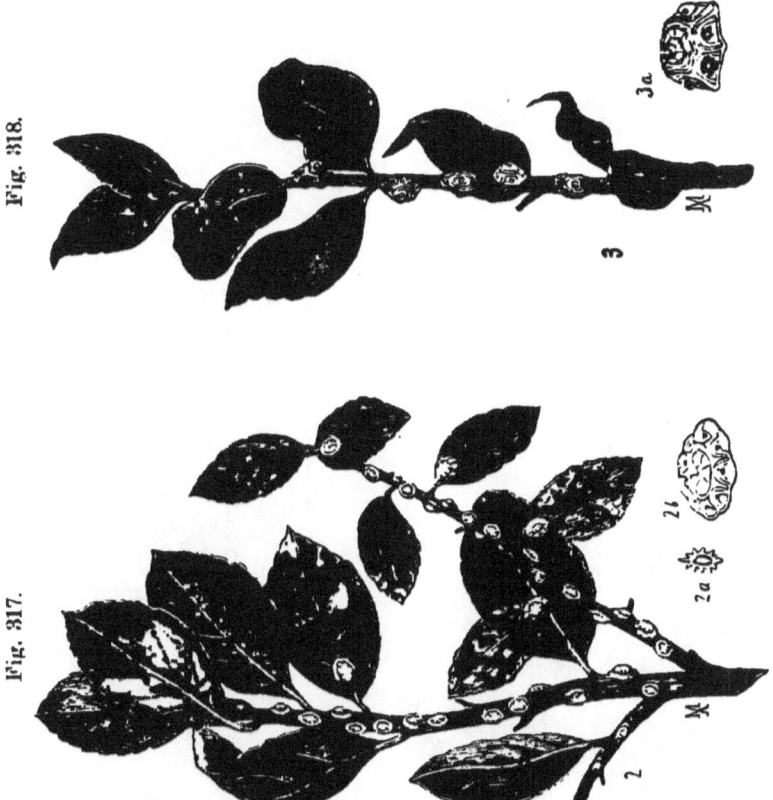

furnished with four digitules, of which the two shortest are very large and horn-shaped. The male of this genus is not known. Examples—the Florida Scale (Fig. 317) and the Barnacle Scale (Fig. 318).

Genus PULVINARIA (Targioni).

This genus is not well defined. It was erected for those species of Lecaninæ, in which the females, after fecundation, secrete below, and at the posterior end of the body, a mass of

cottony material which forms a nidus for the eggs.   Example
—the Cottony Maple Scale (Fig. 319).

Fig. 319.

Genus LECANIUM.

This genus includes those species which are naked and, at first, boat-shaped, taking on, however, after impregnation very diverse forms, from nearly flat to globular.   Examples—

Fig. 320.

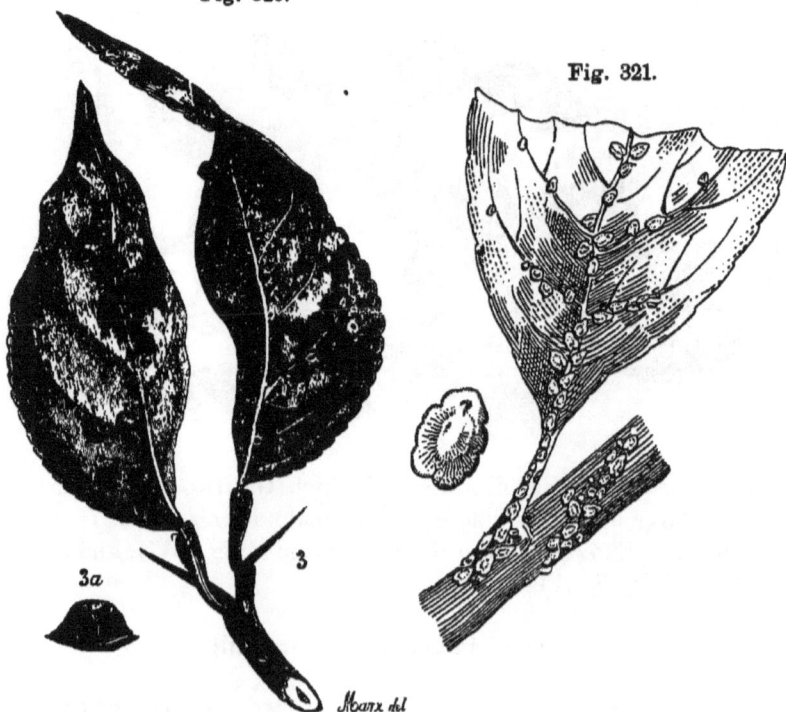

the Black Scale (Fig. 294), the Filbert Scale (Fig. 320), and the Soft Orange Scale (Fig. 321).

SUB-FAMILY III. (*Coccinæ.*)

Genus KERMES (Targioni—Tozzetti).

These insects have the body perfectly globular, or with a slight incision for insertion on the twig or branch. On an external examination no trace of antennæ, legs, or even mouth

Fig. 322.

parts are to be observed, and the insect presents precisely the appearance of a gall. Chiefly found on Oak trees (Fig. 322).

Genus RHIZOCOCCUS (Comstock).

Antennæ of larvæ and of the adult female seven jointed;

ano-genital ring with eight hairs; tarsi of both male and female each with four digitules; margin of body of young and of female in all stages, fringed with tubular spinnerets, which are covered with a waxy excretion. Adult male with a single ocellus behind each eye, and a pair of bristles on each side of the penultimate abdominal segment, each pair supporting a long white filament excreted by numerous pores at its base. The fully developed female makes a dense sac of waxy matter, within which the eggs are laid, and the shriveled body of the insect remains. The full-grown male larva makes a similar sac within which it undergoes its metamorphosis. Example —the Norfolk Island Pine Scale.

Genus DACTYLOPIUS.

The antennæ of the females are six jointed in the larva, and eight jointed in the adult; the male larva has seven jointed antennæ; the tarsi are furnished with four digitules, and the

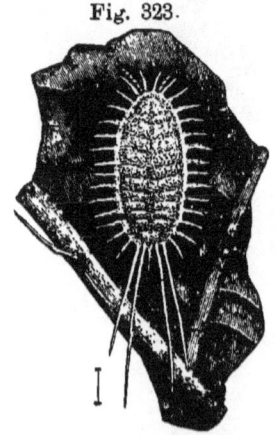

Fig. 323.

Fig. 324.

anal ring with six hairs. Examples—the Mealy Bug with long threads (Fig. 323), and the Destructive Mealy Bug (Fig. 324).

Genus PSEUDOCOCCUS (Westwood).

This genus is very near *Dactylopius*, and nearly all the characters are identical. In the adult female, however, the antennæ are nine jointed, those of the female larva being six jointed and of the male larva seven jointed. The tarsi are not provided with the long digitules, except in *Pseudococcus hederæ*.

Genus Coccus.

The species of this genus may be distinguished from *Dactylopius* and *Pseudococcus* by the following characters:

The antennæ are seven jointed in the adult female, six jointed in the female larva, and five jointed in the male larva. The legs are very slender; the anal ring is destitute of hairs; the eyes are smooth, and there are two ocelli. Example— the Cochineal Insect.

Genus Icerya (Signoret).

Fig. 325.

Antennæ eleven jointed; body covered with a cottony matter of several shades of color, and with a secretion of still longer filaments; skin with rounded spinnerets and with long scattered hairs; antennæ of nearly same size throughout their whole length, and with a long pubescence; the digitules of the claws are elongated and buttoned, those of the tarsi appear as simple hairs; genital apparatus terminating in a tube internally, with a reticulated ring, and without hairs at its extremity. Antennæ of the larva six jointed, with a very long pubescence, and with four hairs upon the last joint much longer than the others; lateral lobes of the extremity of the abdomen with a series of three very long, frequently interlaced bristles. Example—the Cottony Cushion Scale (Figs. 295 and 325).

CHAPTER XXI.

Beneficial Insects.

The greater number of insects feed upon the various parts of plants, and are therefore termed "injurious;" others feed upon decaying animal or vegetable matter, and are called "scavengers;" still others feed upon insects, especially on those which are injurious to plants, and, by thus aiding us in getting rid of these pests, are termed "beneficial insects." Some of this latter kind seize their prey with their jaws, somewhat as a cat catches a mouse, and are hence called "predaceous." To this class belong the Tiger Beetles, which may frequently be seen running over the ground during the hottest part of the day. The one most often met with is the Common Tiger Beetle (Fig. 240), which is of a dull purplish color above, and a bright brassy-green underneath; on each wing-case are three irregular whitish spots. Another species which quite closely resembles the above is the Generous Tiger Beetle (Fig. 241), of a dull purplish color, marked with white as in the figure. The Virginian Tiger Beetle (Fig. 242) is of a dull brownish color. All of the Tiger Beetles have filiform antennæ, and their feet are five jointed. The larvæ of the Tiger Beetles are provided with six legs, and live in holes in the earth. They feed upon Cut-worms and similar insects.

The Ground Beetles also prey upon Cut-worms and other insects, and, like the Tiger Beetles, have filiform antennæ and five jointed feet; but, unlike them, they have horizontal instead of vertical heads. The Gold-spotted Ground Beetle (Fig. 243) is of a brownish color, and on each wing-case are three rows of sunken gold-colored spots.

Another group of predaceous insects are the Lady-birds, which have only three joints in their feet. These insects feed upon Plant-lice, Scale Insects, small caterpillars, etc; the larvæ (Figs. 328, *a*, and 332, *a*,) are provided with six legs, and when fully grown they suspend themselves by the hind part of the body; the skin on the back soon splits open and the pupa (Fig. 328, *b*), by alternately elongating and shortening its body, works the old skin backward until it covers only the posterior part of the pupa, where it is permitted to remain; in due time the skin on the back of the pupa is rent and the pefect beetle (Fig. 328, *c*,) comes forth.

One of the largest kind is the Fifteen-spotted Lady-bird (Fig. 290); it varies in color, from dirty brown to cream color, and the wing-cases are usually marked with fifteen black dots, but the color and markings vary, as shown in the figure

(Fig. 290, *d, e, f* and *g*). The wing-cases of the Thirteen-spotted Lady-bird (Fig. 326) are of a reddish-brown color, and are marked with thirteen black dots. The wing-cases of the Ten-spotted Lady-bird (Fig. 327) are of a pinkish color, and are

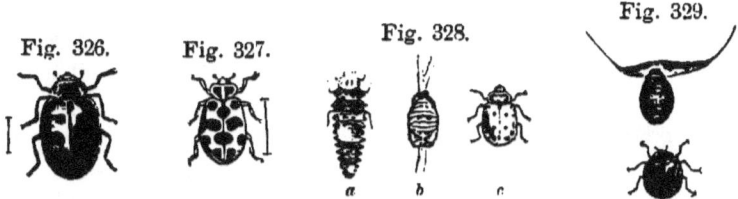

Fig. 326. Fig. 327. Fig. 328. Fig. 329.

marked with ten black dots. The Convergent Lady-bird (Fig. 328, *c*,) has the wing-cases yellowish-brown, and marked with twelve black dots. The Nine-spotted Lady-bird (Fig. 329) has the wing-cases of a yellowish-brown color, marked with nine black dots. The Icy Lady-bird (Fig. 330) has the wing-cases of an orange-yellow color, marked with from four to six black dots. The Trim Lady-bird (Fig. 239) has the wing-cases of an orange-yellow or orange-red color, and unmarked. The California Lady-bird (Fig. 289) differs from the Trim Lady-bird by having a white spot on each of the front corners of the thorax—the Trim Lady-bird having the thorax margined in front and at the sides with yellow. The Twice-

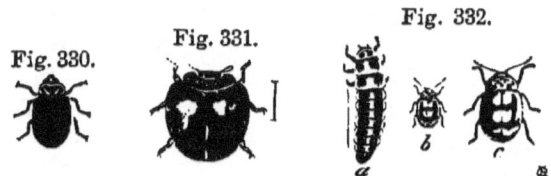

Fig. 330. Fig. 331. Fig. 332.

stabbed Lady-bird (Fig. 331) is entirely black, with the exception of a deep red spot on each wing-case. The Painted Lady-bird (Fig. 332, *c*,) is of a pale yellow color, with a black stripe on each wing-case; the two stripes being connected by two black bands.

The Mantis (Fig. 142) also feeds upon other insects; the female deposits her eggs in large masses (Fig. 308), and the young closely resemble the parents, with the exception of being destitute of wings; they do not pass through a quiet pupa stage, but continue active during their entire lives.

The Soldier Bugs (Figs. 114 and 154) feed upon caterpillars and other insects by impaling them upon their beaks and then leisurely extracting their juices. These bugs do not pass through a quiet pupa state, but continue active from the time they issue from the eggs until they die of old age or some other cause. They do not confine their attacks to insects, but also occasionally feed upon the juices of plants.

The larvæ of the Lace-winged Flies (Fig. 47) feed upon Plant-lice and similar insects. After reaching their full growth, each one spins, in some sheltered place, a globular cocoon, and is soon after changed into a pupa; in due time the pupa comes out of its cocoon and fastens itself to some neighboring object, when the skin on its back soon splits open and the perfect fly (Fig. 22) makes its escape. The female fly deposits her eggs upon the tips of slender thread-like stems (Fig. 22).

The larva of the Syphus-fly (Fig. 231, a,) also feeds upon Plant-lice and similar insects. It is entirely destitute of legs, and after reaching its full growth it attaches itself to the stem of a plant, or some other object, and soon contracts to a pupa (Fig. 231, b), from which the perfect fly (Fig. 231, c), in due time, makes its escape. In pupating, the narrow tapering end of the larva becomes the thickened end of the pupa.

Many kinds of Wasps, such as the Rust-red Wasp (Fig. 183, a), provision their nests with caterpillars, flies, or other insects, to serve as food for their young. Some kinds build nests of mud (Fig. 181); others of a papery substance (Fig. 183, b); still others build their nests in holes in the ground, in decayed wood, or in the stems of plants. The larvæ or young of these Wasps are entirely destitute of legs.

There is a group of insects which, in the larva state, live within the eggs, larvæ or pupæ of other insects, ultimately destroying them; they are commonly called "parasitic" insects. The Ichneumon Flies (Figs. 40, 131 and 134) belong to this class. The female deposits her eggs in the larvæ or pupæ of other insects in which her progeny are to live; from these eggs are hatched small footless grubs, which feed upon the internal parts of the larva and pupa in which the eggs from which they were produced had been deposited by the provident mother. After reaching their full growth some kinds assume the pupa form within the larva or pupa in which they have lived, and the flies, after issuing from the pupa, gnaw holes through the skin of the larva or pupa and make their escape. The larvæ of several kinds, however, first gnaw their way out of the larva or pupa in which they have lived, and then each one spins a cocoon around its body; sometimes they spin a mass of flossy silk, and then crawl into this and spin their cocoons. Occasionally only one parasitic larva lives in a larva or pupa, but sometimes several dozen inhabit one pupa

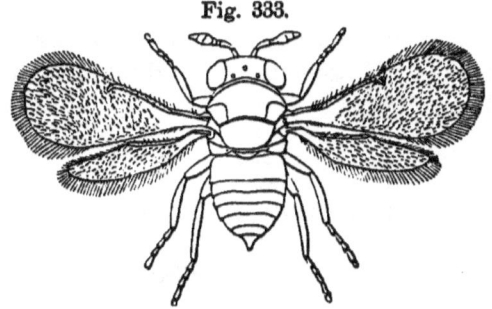

Fig. 333.

or larva. When the egg is deposited in the body of a larva, the larva sometimes assumes the pupa form before the parasitic Ichneumon Fly issues.

Fig. 334.

The Chalcis Flies form another group of insects which live parasitically in the eggs, larvæ or pupæ of other insects; they are very small, and their wings are provided with but few veins (Figs. 333 and 334). They live principally in the eggs of other insects, and many kinds infest various kinds of Scale Insects and Plant-lice.

Another class of parasitic insects is the Tachina Flies (Fig. 236). These flies attach their white eggs to the bodies of caterpillars, etc., and the larvæ which hatch from these eggs gnaw their way into the body of their victim; here they remain until reaching their full growth, when they gnaw their way out and drop to the ground, which they enter and form smooth cells; they do not cast their skins before pupating, but these contract and harden, thus supplying the place of a cocoon. At the proper time the perfect fly (Fig. 236) issues and makes her way to the surface of the earth. This fly very closely resembles the common House Fly, but may at once be distinguished by the slender bristle on the last joint of the antennæ being naked, whereas, in the House Fly this bristle is pectinate, like a feather.

CHAPTER XXII.

Collecting and Preserving Insects.

A cabinet of some kind is almost indispensable to the student of Entomology; in it he should place as many different species of insects as he may be able to obtain from time to time, both by collecting and by exchanging specimens with friends.

One of the chief requisites for successful collecting is a net. The accompanying figure (Fig. 335) illustrates the frame work of a very convenient net, such as is used by Professor Riley, and its construction is thus described by him: "Take two pieces of stout brass wire, each about twenty inches long; bend them half circularly and join at one end by a folding hinge having a check on one side (*b*). The other ends are bent and beaten into two square sockets (*f*) which fit to a nut sunk and soldered into one end of a brass tube (*d*). When so fitted they are secured by a large-headed screw (*e*) threaded to fit into the nut-socket, and with a groove wide enough to receive the back of a common knife blade. The wire hoop is easily detached and folded, as at *c*, for convenient carriage; and the handle may be made of any desired length by cutting a stick and fitting it into the hollow tube *a*, which should be about six inches long."

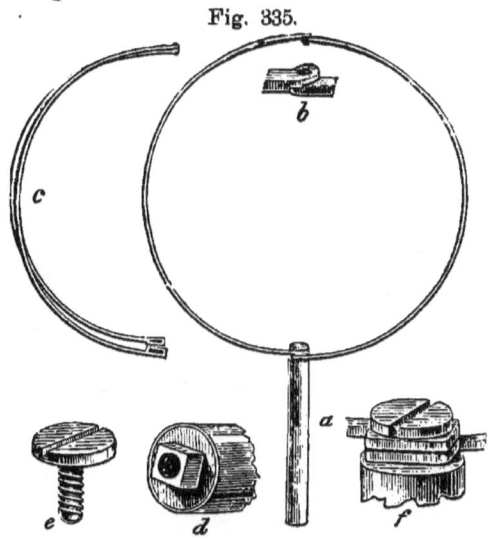

Fig. 335.

A bag of fine gauze or mosquito netting (the finer and stronger the better) should be sewed to a piece of cloth fastened around the wire frame.

Another simpler but less convenient frame (Fig. 336) is thus described by Professor Sanborn: "Make a loop of strong iron or brass wire, of about three sixteenths of an inch in thickness, so that the diameter of the loop or circle will not exceed twelve inches, leaving an inch or an inch and a half of wire at each end bent at nearly right angles. Bind the two extremities together with smaller wire (*a*), and tin them by applying a drop of muriate of zinc, then holding it in the fire or over a gas flame until nearly red hot, when a few grains of block tin or soft solder placed upon them will flow evenly over the whole surface and join them firmly together. Take a Maynard rifle cartridge tube, or any other brass tube of similar

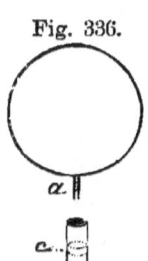

Fig. 336.

dimensions (*b*); if the former, file off the closed end, or perforate it for the admission of the wire, and, having tinned it in the same manner on the inside, push a tight fitting cork half way through (*c*) and pour into it melted tin or soft solder and insert the wires; if carefully done you will have a firmly constructed and very durable foundation for a collecting net. The cork (*c*) being extracted, will leave a convenient socket for inserting a stick or walking cane to serve as a handle."

By attaching a gauze bag to this frame a very handy net will be produced.

For capturing the night-flying moths, many collectors practice what is commonly known as "sugaring." This consists of applying to the trunks of trees, or to strips of cloth attached to the tree, some sweet, attractive and stupefying preparation, such as diluted molasses, or brown sugar, and rum. This is spread upon the trees, etc., in the evening, and by examining these places with a lantern at intervals throughout the night, many moths which could not otherwise be obtained may be collected.

After capturing an insect intended for the cabinet, the next step is to kill it in such a manner as not to injure its form or clothing. For killing most insects the cyanide bottle (Fig. 337) will be all that is needed. This is prepared by putting into a large-mouthed bottle a quantity of the cyanide of potassium (pulverized) equal to a small marble, but the quantity to be issued will depend upon the size of the bottle; pour into the bottle just enough water to dissolve the cyanide, and when this is dissolved drop plaster of paris into the solution until all of the latter is absorbed; now place the bottle in the hot sun, or subject it to artificial heat, until thoroughly dry inside, after which wipe out the inside with a dry rag or piece of

Fig. 337.

paper; now cork the bottle tightly, and in a day or two it will be ready for use. When an insect is thrown into a bottle prepared in this way, and the bottle corked up tightly, the fumes of the cyanide will destroy the insect's life in a very short time. Great care should be exercised in using the cyanide, as it is deadly poison when taken internally, although no serious effect has ever been known to follow the inhaling from the cyanide bottle prepared as directed above, notwithstanding its well known effects upon insect life.

Those insects which are too large to be placed into the cyanide bottle may be killed by the use of chloroform. For this purpose a small and stout bottle, with a brush inserted in the cork (Fig. 338), will be found very serviceable. By moistening the abdomen of the insect with this liquid its life will soon be destroyed.

Fig. 338.

For killing very small and delicate insects, they may be caught in wooden boxes, when, by applying the chloroform to the outside of the box, they will soon become stupefied.

Butterflies, moths and similar insects should not be carried in the cyanide bottle after they are dead, since by rolling around in the bottle, they become more or less denuded of their scales, or otherwise disfigured; as soon as dead they should be taken out of the bottle and pinned into a cork-lined box constructed for this purpose.

In pinning beetles the pin should be thrust through the right wing-case (Fig. 339, a,) so as to come out between the insertion of the middle and the hind pair of legs; bugs should be pinned through the scutellum (Fig. 339, b); all other insects should be pinned through the thorax.

Fig. 339.

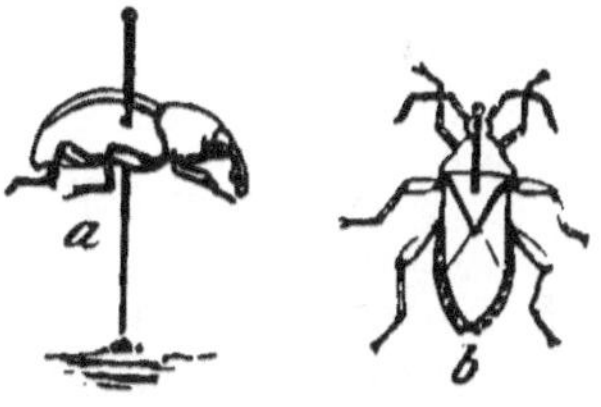

In pinning insects for the cabinet, entomological pins, made expressly for this purpose, should be used; these are made of different sizes ranging from 1 to 10.

the lowest numbers the finest. The No. 2 pins will answer most ordinary purposes. About one third of the length of the pin should be allowed to project above the insect's back.

Small insects, one fourth of an inch in length and under should be gummed to pieces of card-board or to thin plates of mica, through which the pin is afterwards thrust. These are sometimes cut into square pieces, but the better way is to cut the edge into small wedge-shaped teeth, as in Fig. 340.

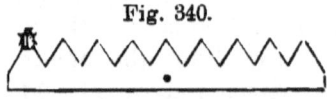

Fig. 340.

For gumming insects upon card-board, etc., Spaulding's liquid glue may be used; or in its stead the following preparation may be used, and is to be preferred:

Pulverized gum tragacanth, three drams; pulverized gum arabic, one dram; corrosive sublimate, one grain; mix, and add a little water.

For spreading out the wings of butterflies, etc., a setting-board of some sort should be used; one that is simple in its construction and answers every purpose is shown at Fig. 341. It is made of two pieces of soft pine boards (the softer the better) about half an inch thick, one and a half inches wide, and of any convenient length; these should be fastened to upright blocks about one and one half inches high at each end, and tapering to one and one sixth inches high at the middle. In fastening the two upper pieces to these, leave a space between the upper pieces wide enough to admit the insect's body; a strip of cork or pith is then glued over this space on the under side, and the work is completed.

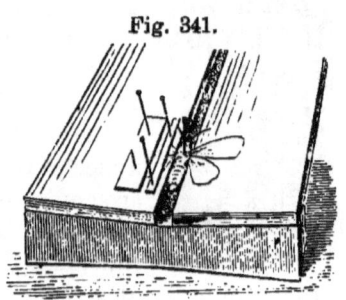

Fig. 341.

Fig. 342.

For stretching out the wings, and for many other purposes, a needle stuck into a wooden handle (Fig. 342) will be found useful; this is made by splitting off a piece of pine wood three or four inches long, then forcing into one end of it the eye end of a common sewing needle; now whittle down the handle to a convenient size and shape (Fig. 342) and the instrument is completed.

For retaining the wings of the insects on the setting board in their proper position, strips of card-board should be pinned over them (Fig. 341), using common short, sharp-pointed pins for this purpose.

The setting-board may then be suspended upon the wall, or it may be placed in a box covered with fine wire gauze or strainer cloth, which will admit plenty of air, while at the same time preventing small insects from gaining access to the specimens. The latter should remain upon the setting-board for at least a month, when they are ready for the cabinet.

Cases for exhibiting insects in, may be made in the form of a shallow box having a tightly fitting lid, in the back of which is fastened a pane of clear glass; they may be of any convenient size, and about two and a half inches deep, inside measurement. The bottom should be lined with thin strips of cork or dry pith, into which to thrust the pins; if pith is used it should first be boiled, to extract the saccharine matter.

If the collection is to be a very extensive one, the cases to contain it may be constructed in the form of two shallow boxes facing each other, and fastened together on one side with hinges, and on the other with hooks and staples; they will then open and shut like a book, and when not in use may be packed away in any convenient place. The boxes may be made of thoroughly seasoned white wood, walnut or cherry. Care should be taken to have the cases or boxes perfectly tight, so as to prevent small insects, mites, etc., from gaining access to and spoiling the collection. The cork or pith in the bottom of the boxes should be covered with white paper, which, if lightly cross-ruled, will greatly facilitate the regular pinning of the specimens.

For relaxing dried insects, place them for twelve or twenty-four hours in a tin box containing a quantity of moistened sand over which a single layer of paper is spread; their wings, etc., can then be easily spread out.

Caterpillars, grubs, pupæ, and similar objects may be preserved in alcohol. They should first be thrown into alcohol diluted with water, and afterwards be removed to vessels containing alcohol of full strength.

Nothing is more annoying to the experienced, or more discouraging to the young collector, than to have his specimens destroyed by mites, or by the larvæ of certain beetles; against the ravages of these pests there is no security. Paste and paper fail to exclude them; camphor is only a partial protector; and the only safeguard is constant vigilance, and the instant destruction of the offenders when observed.

For this purpose many methods have been suggested, such as saturation with turpentine, immersion in alcohol or benzine, exposure in an oven to a heat of 210°, etc., but most of these are liable to injure or even destroy the specimens.

A very good method is to place a galipot or small saucer, containing about twenty-five grains of cyanide of potassium, roughly bruised, with a very little water, in the bottom of the cabinet; drop about six drops of sulphuric acid upon the potassium and close up the cabinet. The gas thus generated will destroy the life of any larva or other insect or animal that may be in the cabinet at the time, as no animate being can inhale this gas and live. Great care should be taken to prevent the inhalation of this gas by the person employing it, as it is highly poisonous.

GLOSSARY.

Abbreviated.—Shortened.
Abdomen.—The posterior division of the body.
Abnormal.—Unnatural; exceptional.
Aculeate.—Prickly.
Acuminate.—Ending in a prolonged point.
Adephagous.—Ravenous; predaceous.
Agamic.—Bringing forth living young, or depositing fertile eggs, without the intervention of the male.
Alula.—A small appendage on the hind edge of the base of the wing in the Two-winged Flies.
Annulated.—Furnished with colored rings.
Antennæ.—The two horn-like appendages to the head (Figs. 89 and 103).
Apex.—The terminal point; the tip.
Apodous.—Destitute of feet.
Approximate.—Near, or near together.
Apterous.—Destitute of wings.
Arista.—A style, or bristle.
Aristate.—Furnished with a bristle.
Articulate.—Divided into joints.
Asexual.—Same as Agamic.
Attenuated.—Tapering.
Aurelia.—Ancient name for pupa.
Base.—The part opposite the apex.
Bi.—Two or twice.

Fig. 343.

Bifid.—Cleft.
Bifurcate.—Two-forked.
Bilobate.—Divided into two lobes.
Bristled antenna.—Fig. 343.

Capitate.—Ending in a head or knob (Figs. 95 and 96).
Carina.—A ridge.
Cauda.—A tail.
Cell.—A term applied to the inclosures made by the veins and cross-veins in the wings (Fig. 125). As these cells differ in number and form in the different insects, they have received different names. In many kinds of Two-winged Flies (such as the Syrphus Fly, Fig. 231, c), the cell next the fore edge of the wing is the *costal* cell; the three back of this, nearest the body, are the first, second and third *basal* cells, and the cell next to the hind edge of the wing is the *anal* cell; toward the outer edge of the wing, from the first basal cell, is the first *posterior* cell, while the three cells back of this, along the margin of the wing, are the second, third and fourth posterior cells; the closed cell between the second basal and the third posterior cells is the *discal* cell (this may easily be known by always being at the lower end of the small cross-vein between the first basal and the first posterior cells); the two cells between the costal and first posterior cells are the *marginal* and *sub-marginal* cells.
Chrysalids.—Plural of chrysalis.
Chrysalis.—The third stage of insect life (Fig. 344; same as pupa).

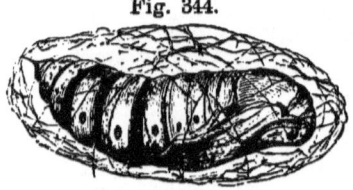

Fig. 344.

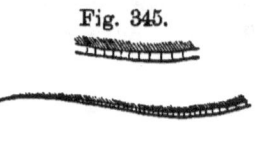

Fig. 345.

Ciliate.—Fringed. (Ciliate antennæ, Fig. 345.)
Cinereous.—Ash-colored.
Clavate.—Enlarged toward the tip (Fig. 92).
Clypeus.—The division of the face immediately above the upper lip.
Coarctate.—Enclosed in the old larva skin.
Cocoon.—A silken case spun by the caterpillar (Fig. 346).

Complete transformation.—When the pupa is incapable of crawling about and of taking food.

Compound eyes.—Placed on each side of the head, and composed of numerous facets or simple eyes placed close together.

Compressed.—Flattened on the sides.

Concolorous.—Of the same color as another part.

Confluent.—Running into each other.

Connate.—United.

Contiguous.—Touching each other.

Cordate.—Heart-shaped.

Coriaceous.—Hard, but flexible.

Corneous.—Horny.

Corrugated.—Wrinkled.

Costa.—Front edge of the wing (Fig. 121, *a*).

Coxa.—A small piece between the thigh and body (Figs. 89 and 103).

Crenate.—Scolloped, the teeth rounded.

Cupreous.—Coppery.

Cylindrical.—Round and long and of the same thickness throughout.

Decumbent.—Bending down.

Deflected.—Bent down.

Dentate.—Toothed.

Depressed.—Flattened from above.

Diffuse.—Spreading.

Digitate.—Divided like the fingers.

Digituli.—Stout hairs, sometimes knobbed at the tip, which occur upon the feet of many kinds of Plant-lice and Scale Insects.

Dilated.—Widened.

Discal.—Relating to the disk.

Discal cell.—A cell situated at the base of the wing in the Butterflies and Moths, but in the Two-winged Flies it is nearest to the outer margin. (See *Cell.*)

Disk.—The upper central part of any given surface.

Fig. 346.

Divaricate.—Spreading apart.
Dorsal.—Relating to the back.

Elliptical.—Elongate-oval.
Elytra.—The hard wing-cases of Beetles.
Emarginate.—Notched.
Epistoma.—The clypeus.
Exserted.—Protruded.
Exuvia.—The cast-off skin.

Falcate.—Sickle-shaped.
Fascia.—A stripe broader than a line.
Fauna.—The animals of any given locality.
Femur.—The thigh (Figs. 89 and 103).
Ferrugineous.—Rust-colored.
Filiform.—Thread-like (Figs. 91 and 94, *a*).
First joint.—The joint farthest from the tip; the basal joint.
Flabellate antenna.—Fig. 347.
Flavescent.—Yellowish.
Flexuous.—Waving; zigzag.
Fovea.—A pit or rounded depression.
Frenulum.—A bristle on the front edge of the hind wing which fits into a hook beneath the front wing, uniting the wings during flight. (See Fig. 122, *fr.*)
Fuliginous.—Smoky.
Fulvous.—Tawny, reddish yellow.
Furcate.—Forked.
Fuscous.—Dark brown.
Fusiform.—Spindle-shaped; tapering toward both ends (Fig. 93.)

Ganglion.—A swelling in the nervous cord.
Geminate.—In pairs.
Geniculate.—Elbowed (Fig. 348).
Genus.—A class or group, each member of which possesses certain characters not found in those individuals which belong to a different class or group.
Glabrous.—Smooth.

Fig. 347.

Fig. 348.

Glaucous.—Bluish-green.
Granulated.—Covered with small rounded elevations.
Gregarious.—Living in flocks or communities.
Halteres.—Small thread-like organs which terminate in a knob, taking the place of the hind pair of wings in the Two-winged Flies.
Haustellate.—Furnished with a beak or proboscis.
Hemelytra.—The front wings of the True Bugs.
Hermaphrodite.—An individual in which both the male and the female organs occur.
Heteromerous.—Having five joints in the front and middle feet, and only four joints in the hind ones.
Hexapod.—Six footed.
Hirsute.—Clothed with stiff hairs.
Humerus.—Anterior outer angle of the wing-cases of Beetles.
Hyaline.—Transparent, like glass.
Hyperstoma.—The clypeus in the Two-winged Flies.

Imago.—The adult or perfect insect (Fig. 349).
Imbricated.—Over-lapping, like the shingles on a roof.
Immaculate.—Spotless.
Immarginate.—Without an elevated margin.
Incomplete transformation.—When the pupa is capable of crawling about and of taking food.
Incrassated.—Thickened.
Incumbent.—Lying upon.
Infuscated.—Darkened with a blackish tinge.

Fig. 349.

Joint.—A node or part between two joints; in this sense, that part of the arm which is between the joints of the elbow and wrist would be called a joint.

Labial palpi.—Small jointed appendages of the lower lip (Fig. 103).
Labium.—The lower lip.

Lamelliform.—Leaf-like.
Lamellate.—With flattened plates (Fig. 100).
Lamina.—A plate or sheet-like piece.
Larva.—The second stage of insect life, or that immediately following the egg (Fig. 350; such as grubs, caterpillars, maggots, etc.).

Fig. 350.

Lateral.—On one side.
Line.—One twelfth of an inch (Fig. 351); a very narrow stripe.

Fig. 351.

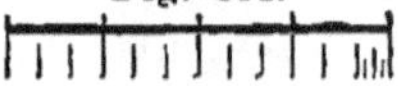

Linear.—Long and narrow and of equal width.
Lingula.—The tongue.
Lunate.—Half-moon shaped.
Luteous.—Deep yellow.

Maculate.—Spotted.
Mandibles.—The upper jaws, placed between the upper lip and the lower jaws (Fig. 103).
Mandibulate.—Provided with jaws.
Maxillæ.—The lower jaws, placed between the upper jaws and the lower lip (Fig. 103).
Membraneous.—Thin; parchment-like.
Mentum.—The chin (Fig. 103).
Mesothorax.—That division of the thorax to which the middle pair of legs are attached (Fig. 89).
Metamorphoses.—Same as *Transformations*.
Metathorax.—That division of the thorax to which the hind pair of legs are attached (Fig. 89).
Moniliform.—Like a string of beads.
Mucronate.—Ending in a sharp point.

Normal.—Natural; usual.
Nymph.—Ancient name for pupa.

Obsolete.—Indistinct.
Obtected.—Not enclosed in the old larva skin.
Occiput.—Hind part of the head.
Ocelli.—Simple eyes, usually placed on the top of the head.
Ocellus.—A simple eye (Fig. 89).

Ochreous.—A more or less deep ochre-yellow color.
Olivaceous.—Olive colored.
Orbicular.—Nearly circular (Fig. 121, *mo*).
Oval.—Egg-shaped.
Ovate.—More or less egg-shaped.
Oviparous.—Producing eggs.
Oviposition.—Act of depositing eggs.
Ovipositor.—The instrument by which the female lays her eggs.

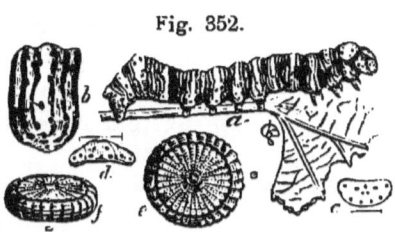

Fig. 352.

Ovum.—An egg (Fig. 352, *e* and *f*).

Palmate.—Hand-shaped.
Palpi.—Feelers attached to the lower lip and the lower jaws (Figs. 89 and 103).
Parasitic.—Living in or upon another animal.
Parthenogenesis.—Bringing forth living young or depositing fertile eggs without the previous intervention of the male.
Patagia.—The shoulder tufts (Fig. 123, *m*).
Pectinate.—Comb-toothed (Fig. 115, *a*).
Peduncle.—A stem.
Pentamerous.—Having five joints in all the feet.
Penultimate.—The last but one.
Perfoliate.—Flattened joints or plates with the stem apparently passing through their centers (as the terminal part of Fig. 98).
Petiolate.—Supported on a stem.
Piceous.—Pitchy black.
Pile.—Hair; usually hair arranged in rows.
Pilose.—Clothed with long flexible hairs.
Plumose.—Like a feather.
Poisers.—Same as *Halteres*.
Porrect.—Straight out.
Prismatic.—Three sided, like a prism.
Proboscis.—The beak or sucker.
Process.—A projection.
Pro-legs.—The fleshy legs of caterpillars.

GLOSSARY.

Prothorax.—The first division of the thorax to which the first pair of legs is attached (Fig. 89). (In the Beetles, Bugs, Grasshoppers, and similar insects, this part is commonly termed the *thorax*.)

Pruinose.—Frosted; covered with a whitish powder.

Pterostigma.—Same as *Stigma*.

Pubescent.—Clothed with very fine hair or down.

Pulvilli.—Small cushions beneath the feet of the Two-winged Flies.

Punctured.—Marked with minute impressed dots, as if pricked with the point of a pin.

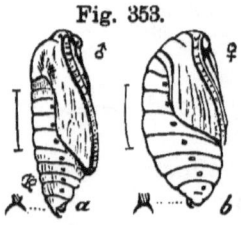

Fig. 353.

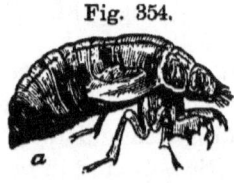

Fig. 354.

Pupa.—Same as *Chrysalis*. (The latter term is usually applied to such as are incapable of moving about (Fig. 353); while those which are active (Fig. 354) are commonly called *Pupæ*.

Pupate.—To assume the pupa form.

Quadrate.—Square, or nearly so.

Raptorial.—Adapted for seizing prey.

Reniform.—Kidney shaped (Fig. 121, *mr*).

Reticulated.—Like net-work.

Rostrum.—Beak.

Rufescent.—Somewhat reddish.

Rufous.—Reddish.

Rugose.—Wrinkled.

Saltatory.—Leaping.

Sanguineous.—Blood-red.

Scabrous.—Roughened with projecting points.

Scrobe.—A groove at the base of the antenna.

Scutel.—A triangular piece between the base of the wing-covers and the thorax.
Segments.—The parts into which an insect's body is divided by the transverse impressed lines or circles (Fig. 352, *b*).
Sericeous.—Like silk.
Serrate.—Saw-toothed (Fig. 97).
Sessile.—Attached by the whole width.
Seta.—A bristle.
Setaceous.—Bristle-like.
Smooth.—Not roughened nor spined.
Spinnerets.—Small openings out of which silk and other secretions are excreted. (In caterpillars they are situated in the lower lip, but in the Scale Insects they are situated on various parts of the abdomen.
Spinous.—Furnished with spines.
Spiracles.—The breathing pores or external openings of the wind-pipe (tracheæ.) (Fig. 89.)
Spurs.—Thick spines.
Stemmata.—Same as *Ocelli*.
Stigma.—A thickened spot on the front edge of the fore wings (Fig. 126, 7).
Stigmata.—A term applied to the orbicular and reniform spots on the front wings of Moths. (See Fig. 121, *mo* and *mr*.)
Striæ.—Impressed lines or grooves.
Striate.—Marked with impressed lines; grooved.
Sturnum.—The underside of the thorax.
Sulcate.—Grooved.
Suture.—The place where the two parts meet.

Tarsi.—Feet.
Tawny.—A pale dirty yellow.
Tegmina.—The front wings of Grasshoppers.
Tergum.—The upper side of the abdomen.
Tessellated.—Checkered.
Testaceous.—Pale dull red.
Tetramerous.—Having four joints in all the feet.
Thorax.—That division of the body to which the legs and wings are attached.

Tibia.—The shank or shin; that part of the leg between the thigh and foot (Fig. 103).
Tomentose.—Covered with fine matted hairs.
Trachea.—The wind-pipe.
Transformations.—Changes; such as changing from a larva to a pupa, or from a pupa to a perfect insect.

Fig. 355.

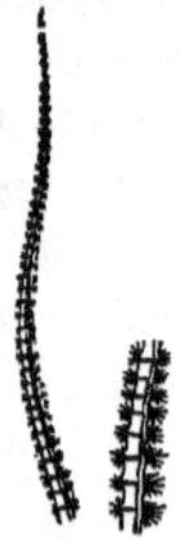

Transverse.—Crosswise.
Trimerous.—Having three joints in all the feet.
Trochanter.—An appendage at the base of the thigh (Fig. 89).
Trophi.—The mouth parts.
Truncate.—Cut squarely off.
Tubercle.—A small swelling or prominence.
Tuberculate.—Furnished with tubercules.
Tufted antennæ.—Fig. 355.

Uncinate.—Hooked at the tip.

Venter.—The underside of the body.
Verticillate.—In whorles.
Villous.—Clothed with long soft hairs.
Vitta.—A colored stripe running lengthwise.
Viviparous.—Bringing forth living young.

CORRECTIONS.

By an oversight, several typographical errors will be found in pages 81 to 96, the principal of which are as follows:

Page 81, line 3; for *Sectlon*, read *Section*.
Page 85, line 16; insert a parenthesis before *including*.
Page 86, line 14; for *body*, read *latter*.
Page 87, Fig. 250; insert a period after 250.
Page 88, line 2; insert *and* before the second *the*.
Page 91, line 15; insert a comma after *animals*.
Page 91, foot-note; for *larva*, read *larvæ*.
Page 92, line 33; for *is*, read *are*.
Page 93, line 1; for *Melœ* read *Meloe*.
Page 93, line 4; for *possesses*, read *possess*.
Page 93, line 22; for *Ground*, read *Darkling*.
Page 94, line 4; for *Beetles*, read *Beetle*.
Page 94, line 7; for *Tetremera*, read *Tetramera*.

INDEX.

Aberrant Wood Beetle, 91.
Achemon Sphinx, *Philampelis achemon*, 43, 54, 65.
Acrididæ, 111.
Aegeridæ, 66.
Agrionidæ, 113.
Aleurodidæ, 101.
Ambulatoria, 108, 110.
American Currant Borer, *Psenocerus supernotatus*, 97.
American Procris, *Procris Americana*, 68.
Annelida, 3.
Anthicidæ, 93.
Anthomyia calopteni, 80.
Ant-lion, *Myrmeleon*, 49, 113.
Ants, 57.
Aphaniptera, 53.
Aphididæ, 100.
Aphodidæ, 87.
Apidæ, 54.
Apple Curculio, *Anthonomus quadrigibbus*, 95.
Apple Maggot, *Trypeta pomonella*, 47.
Apple-tree Aphis, *Aphis mali*, 31, 45.
Arachnida, 2, 3.
Archippus Butterfly, *Danais Archippus*, 17, 63.
Army Worm, *Leucania unipuncta*, 9, 10.

Articulata, 1, 2.
Ash-colored Blister Beetle, *Macrobasis unicolor*, 93.
Asparagus Beetle, *Crioceris asparagi*, 48.
Aspidiotus, 115, 116, 117.
Back-boned Animals, 1.
Bacon Beetle, *Dermestes lardarius*, 85.
Banded Robber, *Milyas cinctus*, 106.
Bark Beetles, 93.
Bark-lice, 103, 114.
Barnacle Scale, *Ceroplastes cirripediformis*, 121.
Bean Weevil, *Bruchus obsoletus*, 95.
Beautiful Wood-nymph, *Eudryas grata*, 68.
Bed Bugs, *Cimex lectularius*, 53, 107.
Bees, 14, 16, 30, 54.
Beetles, 5, 9, 16, 29, 35, 50, 80.
Belostoma, 47.
Bembecidæ, 56.
Bird-lice, 108.
Black Burying Beetle, *Silpha inæqualis*, 85.
Black Horse-fly, *Tabanus atratus*, 77.
Black Melanactes, *Melanactes piceus*, 91.

Black Scale, *Lecanium oleæ*, 103, 122.
Blattidæ, 109.
Blister Beetles, 21, 92.
Blow Flies, 79.
Body Lice, *Pediculus corporis*, 53.
Bombycidæ, 48, 68.
Bordered Plant Bug, *Largus succinctus*, 107.
Borers, 9.
Bot-flies, 78.
Brachycera, 76, 77.
Bracon Fly, 57.
Bran Beetle, *Silvanus quadricollis*, 86.
Branch and Twig Burrower, *Polycaon confertus*, 91.
Branch Borer, *Bostrichus bicaudatus*, 91.
Branch Borers, 91.
Brasslets, 58.
Bristly Cut Worm, *Mamestra renigera*, 71.
Broad-necked Prionus, *Prionus laticollis*, 48, 80.
Brown Grasshoppers, 111.
Bruchidæ, 94.
Bruchus Weevils, 94.
Bud Worm, *Penthina oculana*, 74.
Buffalo Tree-hopper, *Ceresa bubalus*, 8, 44, 103.
Bugs, 28, 30.
Bumble Bees, *Bombus*, 55.
Buprestidæ, 90.
Buprestis Beetles, 90.
Burying Beetles, 85.
Butterflies, 5, 7, 9, 14, 16, 28, 30, 60, 61.

Cabbage Aphis, *Aphis brassicæ*, 10′.
Cabbage Bug, *Strachia histrionica*, 48.
Cabbage Maggot, *Anthomyia brassicæ*, 86.
Cabbage Plusia, *Plusia brassicæ*, 71
Caddis Flies, 113.
California Grape-vine Hopper, *Erythroneura comes*, 103.
California Lady-bird, *Coccinella 5-notata var. Californica*, 99, 127.
Camellia Scale, *Uhleria camelliæ*, 120.
Canker Worm, 15.
Cantharis, 93.
Capsidæ, 107.
Carabidæ, 82.
Cecidomyidæ, 76.
Cecropia Moth, *Samia cecropia*, 11, 70.
Centipedes, 2, 4.
Cerambycidæ, 97.
Cercopidæ, 103.
Ceroplastes, 120.
Cetonians, 88.
Cetonidæ, 88.
Chalcididæ, 58.
Chalcis Flies, 58, 129.
Cherry-leaf Roller, *Cacœcia cerasivorana*, 74.
Cherry-tree Borer, *Dicerca divaricata*, 90.
Chestnut-bud Beetle, *Pityophthorus pubipennis*, 96.
Chicken-lice, *Goniocotes burnetti*, 53.

Chigoe, *Sarcopsylla penetrans*, 77.
Chinch Bug, *Micropus leucopterus*, 15, 21, 106.
Chionaspis, 115, 117.
Chionaspis ortholobis, 117.
Chionea, 77.
Chrysididæ, 57.
Chrysomelidæ, 98.
Cicada, 35.
Cicadidæ, 104.
Cicindelidæ, 81.
Cistelidæ, 93.
Citrus Scale, *Mytilaspis citricola*, 119.
Clams, 2.
Clavicornes, 81, 83.
Clear-winged Moths, 66.
Clothes Moth, *Tinea flavifrontella*, 75.
Clover-hay Worm, *Asopia costalis*, 73.
Coccidæ, 101, 114.
Coccinæ, 115, 122.
Coccinellidæ, 99.
Coccus, 124.
Cochineal Insect, *Coccus carti*, 124.
Cockroaches, 109.
Codlin Moth, *Carpocapsa pomonella*, 9, 74.
Coleoptera, 26, 38, 48, 49, 50, 80.
Colorado Potato Beetle, *Doryphora 10-lineata*, 98.
Common Fire-fly, *Photinus pyralis*, 92.
Common Tiger Beetle, *Cicindela vulgaris*, 82, 125.

Convergent Lady-bird, *Hippodamia convergens*, 126.
Copper Butterflies, 63.
Copridæ, 87.
Coreidæ, 106.
Corn Worm, *Heliothis armigera*, 71.
Cottony Cushion Scale, *Icerya purchasi*, 103, 125.
Cottony Maple Scale, *Pulvinaria innumerabilis*, 121.
Crabronidæ, 56.
Crabs, 1, 2, 23.
Crane Flies, 47, 77.
Crickets, 30, 35, 108, 110.
Crustacea, 2.
Cuckoo Bees, 55.
Cucujidæ, 86.
Cucujus Beetles, 86.
Cucumber Flea-beetle, *Epitrix cucumeris*, 99.
Culicidæ, 76.
Curculionidæ, 95.
Currant Span Worm, *Eufitchia ribearia*, 72.
Cursoria, 108, 109.
Cut-worms, 126.
Cynipidæ, 58.
Dactylopius, 124.
Dakruma coccidivora, 43.
Darkling Beetles, 39, 94.
DeLong's Moth, *Clisiocampa constricta*, 8, 57.
Dermestidæ, 85.
Destructive Mealy Bug, *Dactylopius destructor*, 124.
Diaspinæ, 114, 115.
Diaspis, 115, 116, 118.
Digger Wasps, 56.

Diptera, 36, 47, 48, 76.
Dissimilar-winged Bugs, 105.
Divers, 82.
Dotted-legged Plant-bug, *Euschistus variolarius*, 44, 52.
Dragon Flies, 30, 41, 51, 111, 112.
Dytiscidæ, 82.
Earth-worms, 3.
Earwig, *Forficula auricularia*, 9, 40, 41, 48, 109.
Egg Parasites, 57.
Eight-spotted Forester, *Alypia octomaculata*, 68.
Elateridæ, 90.
Ephemeridæ, 112.
Epicauta, 93.
Fall Canker-worm, *Anisopteryx autumnata*, 43, 72.
False Chinch-bug, *Nysius destructor*, 106.
Field Crickets, 110.
Fifteen-spotted Lady-bird, *Mysia 15-punctata*, 99, 126.
Figure 8 Minor Moth, *Mamestra renigera*. 71.
Filbert Scale, *Lecanium hemisphæricum*, 122.
Filicornes, 81.
Fiorinia, 120.
Fire-flies, 92.
Flat-headed Apple-tree Borer, *Chrysobothris femorata*, 11, 16, 39, 90.
Fleas, 53, 77.
Flesh Flies, 6, 79, 80.
Florida Scale, *Ceroplastes floridensis*, 121.
Forficularidæ, 109.

Formicidæ, 57.
Four-footed Butterflies, 62.
Frosted Leaf-hopper, *Pæciloptera pruinosa*, 104.
Fulgoridæ, 104.
Fungus Flies, 112.
Galgula Bugs, 105.
Galgulidæ, 105.
Gall Flies, 8, 58.
Gall Gnats, 76.
Generous Tiger Beetle, *Cicindela generosa*, 82, 125.
Geometers, 14.
Geometrid Moths, 71.
Geotrupidæ, 87.
Glassy Cut-worm, *Hadena devastatrix*, 11, 12.
Gnawing Insects, 36, 50.
Golden-eyed Flies. *Hemerobius*, 113.
Golden Wasps, 57.
Goldsmith Beetle, *Cotalpa lanigera*, 2.
Gold-spotted Ground Beetle, *Calosoma calidum*, 82, 126.
Gooseberry Fruit Moth, *Pempelia grossulariæ*, 73.
Grain Aphis, *Siphonophora avenæ*, 31, 44, 101.
Grain Moth. *Gelechia cerealella*, 75.
Grape Curculio, 8.
Grape-leaf Folder, *Desmia maculalis*, 73.
Grape Phylloxera, *Phylloxera vastatrix*, 76.
Grape Plume Moth, *Pterophorus periscelidactylus*, 75.

Grape-seed Maggot, *Isosoma vitis*, 38.
Grape-vine Beetles, 88.
Graspers, 108, 109.
Grasshoppers, 8, 9, 20, 23, 30, 108.
Gray Tree-cricket, *Œcanthus latipennis*, 8.
Green Fruit Beetle, *Allorhina nitida*, 89.
Green Grasshoppers, 110.
Ground Beetles, 12, 82, 126.
Grouse Locusts, 111.
Gryllidæ, 110.
Gyrinidæ. 83.
Harlequin Cabbage-bug, *Strachia histrionica*, 15, 45.
Harris' Scale, *Chionaspis furfurus*, 118.
Harvest Flies, 35, 104.
Haustellata, 36, 42.
Hawk Moths, 64.
Head Lice, *Pediculus capitis*, 53.
Helophilus, 47.
Hemerobidæ, 113.
Hemiptera, 36, 44, 48, 100, 105.
Hesperidæ, 63.
Hessian Fly, *Cecidomyia destructor*, 5, 9, 11, 76.
Heterocera, 60, 64.
Heteromera, 80, 92.
Heteroptera, 36, 46, 105.
Hickory Borer, *Chion cinctus*, 97.
Homoptera, 36, 44, 100.
Honey Bees, *Apis mellifica*, 55.
Hop Aphis, *Phorodon humuli*, 45.

Hornet, *Vespa maculata*, 51.
Horn Tails, 59.
Horse Bot-fly, *Œstrus equi*, 53, 78.
Horse Flies, 28, 77.
House Flies, 14, 79.
House Fly, *Musca domestica*, 79, 129.
Hydrometridæ, 105.
Hydrophilidæ, 84.
Hymenoptera, 36, 37, 48, 49, 50, 54.
Icerya, 125.
Ichneumon Flies, 8, 33, 37, 57, 112, 128.
Ichneumonidæ, 57.
Icy Lady-bird, *Hippodamia glacialis*, 127.
Imported Cabbage Butterfly, *Pieris rapæ*, 50, 61.
Imported Currant Saw-flies, *Nematus ventricosus*, 7, 13, 37.
Imported Grape Flea-beetle, *Adoxus vitis*, 99.
Indian Cetonia, *Euryomia inda*, 89.
Insecta, 2.
Isabella Moth, *Pyrrharctia isabella*, 70.
Jigger, *Sarcopsylla penetrans*. 77.
Jointed Animals, 1.
Joint Worms, *Isosoma hordei*, 9.
Julus, 2.
Jumpers, 109, 110.
Jumping Plant-lice, 103.
June Beetle, *Phyllophaga fusca*, 40.

June Beetles, 87.
Katydid, *Platyphyllum concamum*, 7, 35, 40, 51, 110.
Kermes, 122.
Lace-winged Flies, 5, 8, 10, 21, 42, 49, 113, 127.
Lady Birds, 99, 126.
Lamellicornes, 81, 87.
Lampyridæ, 92.
Land Scavenger Beetles, 84.
Lantern Flies, 104.
Large Darkling Grape Beetle, *Eleodes quadricollis*, 94.
Leaf-cutting Bees, *Megachile*, 55.
Leaf-hoppers, 103.
Leaf-miners, 74.
Leaf-rollers, 73.
Lecaninæ, 115, 120.
Lecanium, 121.
Lemon-peel Scale, *Aspidiotus nerii*, 103, 116.
Lepidoptera, 36, 42, 49, 50, 60.
Libellulidæ, 112.
Lice, 47, 108.
Lightning Beetles, 92.
Lobsters, 2, 23.
Locustidæ, 110.
Locusts, 111.
Locust-tree Borer, *Clytus robiniæ*, 97.
Long-horned Borers, 48, 96, 97.
Long-horned Flies, 76.
Long-toed Water Beetles, 83.
Lucanidæ, 86.
Lycænidæ, 48, 63.
Lygæidæ, 106.
Lytta, 93.
Mallophagidæ, 108.

Mandibulata, 26, 50.
Mantidæ, 109.
Mantis, *Mantis carolina*, 40, 109, 127.
Many-banded Robber, *Milyas cinctus*, 44.
Margined Water Beetle, *Dytiscus marginalis*, 82.
May Flies, 21, 111, 112.
Meal Worm, *Tenebrio obscurus*, 94.
Mealy Bugs, 114.
Mealy Bug with long threads, *Dactylopius longifilis*, 124.
Mealy-winged Bugs, 101.
Measuring-worms, 14, 49, 72.
Melandryidæ, 93.
Meloë, 39, 93.
Meloidæ, 92.
Melolonthidæ, 87.
Membranaceidæ, 107.
Millipedes, 2, 4.
Mites, 2, 3.
Mole Crickets, 110.
Mollusca, 2.
Monilicornes, 81, 86.
Mosquito, 35, 76.
Moths, 5, 16, 28, 30, 60, 64.
Muscidæ, 79.
Museum Beetles, 85.
Myriapoda, 2, 4.
Mytilaspis, 115, 118.
Narcissus Fly, *Merodon narcissi*, 78.
Native Currant Saw-fly, *Pristophora grossulariæ*, 10, 59.
Negro Bug, *Corimelæna pulicaria*, 107.
Nemocera, 76.

Nepidæ, 105.
Neuroptera, 36, 41, 49, 50, 111.
Nine-spotted Lady-bird, *Coccinella 9-notata*, 127.
Noctuidæ, 70.
Norfolk Island Pine Scale, *Rhizococcus araucariæ*, 123.
Notonectidæ, 105.
Notoxus Beetles, 93.
Nymphalidæ, 62.
Nyssonidæ, 56.
Odonata, 112.
Œstridæ, 78.
Onion Fly, *Anthomyia ceparum*, 47.
Orchard Tent-caterpillar Moth, *Clisiocampa americana*, 8, 42.
Orthoptera, 36, 40, 48, 50, 108.
Owlet Moths, 70.
Ox Bot-fly, *Œstrus bovis*, 48, 78.
Painted Lady-bird, *Harmonia picta*, 127.
Panorpidæ, 113.
Papilionidæ, 61.
Parasitic Beetles, 92.
Parlatoria, 115, 119.
Parnidæ, 83.
Parsley Worm, *Papilio asterias*, 49.
Peach-tree Borer, *Ægeria exitiosa*, 66.
Pear Slug, *Selandria cerasi*, 49.
Pear-tree Psylla, *Psylla pyri*, 103.
Pear-tree Scolytus, *Xyleborus pyri*, 96.

Pea Weevil, *Bruchus pisi*, 95.
Pecticornes, 81, 86.
Pediculidæ, 108.
Pentamera, 80, 81.
Pergande's Orange Scale, *Parlatoria pergandii*, 120.
Perla Flies, 112.
Perlidæ, 112.
Phalænidæ, 71.
Phasmidæ, 110.
Phryganidæ, 113.
Phylloxera Mite, *Tyroglyphus Phylloxeræ*, 4.
Pieridæ, 61.
Pirate Bugs, 105.
Plant Beetles, 97.
Plant bugs, 20, 107.
Plant-lice, 23, 30, 31, 100, 126, 127, 128.
Plum Curculio, *Conotrachelus nenuphar*, 8, 11, 16, 95.
Plume Moths, 75.
Plum Gouger, *Anthonomus prunicida*, 95.
Pompilidæ, 56.
Potato Flea-beetle, *Epitrix subcrinita*, 99.
Potato Moth, *Gelechia sp.?* 75.
Potato-stalk Weevil, *Pseudobaris trinotatus*, 95.
Predaceous Ground Beetles, 81.
Predaceous Water Beetles, 82.
Prickly Bark Beetle, *Leptostylus aculiferus*, 51.
Prionus Beetle, *Prionus laticollis*, 16.
Proctotrupidæ, 57.
Pseudococcus, 124.

Pseudococcus hederæ, 124.
Pseudo-neuroptera, 42.
Psocidæ, 112.
Psocus, 41.
Psyllidæ, 103.
Pterophoridæ, 75.
Ptinidæ, 91.
Pulicidæ, 77.
Pulvinaria, 121.
Pyralidæ, 73.
Quince Curculio, *Conotrachelus cratægi*, 95.
Radiata, 2.
Raptoria, 108, 109.
Raspberry Borer, *Agrilus ruficollis*, 90.
Raspberry-root Borer, *Ægeria marginata*, 66.
Raw-hide Beetle, *Dermestes lardarius*, 85.
Red Scale, *Aspidiotus aurantii*, 116.
Red Scale of Florida, *Aspidiotus ficus*, 116.
Red-shouldered Grape-vine Borer, *Sinoxylon basilare*, 91.
Red Spider, *Tetranchus telarius*, 2.
Reduvidæ, 105.
Red-winged Wasp, *Priocnemis sp?* 56.
Rhizococcus, 123.
Rhopalocera, 60, 61.
Ring-banded Soldier-bug, *Perillus circumcinctus*, 44.
Rose Aphis. *Siphonophora rosæ*, 31.
Rose Chafer, *Macrodactylus subspinosus*, 88.

Rose Saw-fly, *Selandria rosæ*, 38.
Rose Scale, *Diaspis rosæ*, 117.
Round-headed Apple-tree Borer, *Saperda candida*, 11, 97.
Rove Beetles, 41, 49, 86, 96.
Runners, 108, 109.
Rust-red Wasp, *Polistes rubiginosus*, 56, 128.
Rutelidæ, 88.
Saltatoria, 109, 110.
Sand Wasps, 56.
Satellitia Sphinx, *Philampelis pandorus*, 65.
Saw-flies, 8, 33, 49, 59.
Saw-horned Borers, 48, 89.
Scale Bugs, 114.
Scale Insects, 43, 45, 101, 114, 126.
Scarabæidæ, 87.
Scolytidæ, 96.
Scorpions, 4.
Scorpion Flies, 113.
Scurfy Scale, *Chionaspis furfurus*, 118.
Scutelleridæ, 107.
Semicolon Butterfly, *Grapta interrogationis*, 42.
Serricornes, 81, 89.
Seventeen-year Locust, *Cicada septemdecim*, 104.
Sheep Bot-fly, *Œestrus ovis*, 78.
Sheep Scab-mite, *Psoroptes equi*, 4.
Short-horned Borers, 96.
Short-horned Flies, 76, 77.
Short-toed Water Beetles, 84.
Sialidæ, 113.

Sialis Flies, 113.
Silk Worm, *Sericaria mori*, 70.
Silphidæ, 85.
Similar-winged Bugs, 100.
Skip-jacks, 91.
Skippers, 63.
Slugs, 2.
Small Darkling Grape Beetle, *Blapstinus lecontei*, 94.
Snails, 2.
Snout Beetles, 95.
Snout Moths, 73.
Snowy Tree-cricket, *Œcanthus niveus*, 8.
Soft-bodied Animals, 2.
Soft Orange Scale, *Lecanium hesperidum*, 122.
Soft-winged Beetles, 91.
Soldier Bugs, 9, 48, 107, 127.
Southern Cabbage Butterfly, *Pieris protodice*, 50.
Spanish Fly, *Cantharis vesicatoria*, 93.
Span-worms, 12, 13, 49, 72.
Sphingidæ, 64.
Spiders, 1, 2, 3.
Spined Soldier-bug, *Podisus spinosus*, 44, 53, 107.
Spinners, 68.
Spotted Pelidnota, *Pelidnota punctata*, 88.
Spring Beetles, 90.
Spring Canker-worm, *Anisopteryx vernata*, 43, 72.
Squash Bug, *Coreus tristis*, 47, 106.
Stable Flies, *Stomoxys calcitrans*, 79.
Stag Beetles, 86.

Stalk Borer, *Gortyna nitela*, 71.
Staphylinidæ, 86.
Star-fishes, 2.
Steel-blue Flea-beetle, *Graptodera chalybea*, 98.
Strawberry-crown Borer, *Analcis fragariæ*, 96.
Strawberry Leaf-roller, *Phoxopteris fragariæ*, 74.
Strawberry Saw-fly, *Emphytus maculatus*, 38.
Striped Blister Beetle, *Epicauta vittata*, 93.
Striped Cucumber Beetle, *Diabrotica vittata*, 40, 99.
Sucking Insects, 36, 42.
Swallow-tails, 61.
Syrphidæ, 77.
Syrphus Flies, 14, 77, 128.
Tabanidæ, 77.
Tachina Flies, 79, 129.
Tarantula Hawks, *Pompilus formosus*, 57.
Tawny Emperor Butterfly, *Apatura clyton*, 62.
Tenebrionidæ, 94.
Ten-lined Leaf Eater, *Polyphylla 10-lineata*, 88.
Ten-spotted Lady-bird, *Hippodamia maculata*, 126.
Tenthredinidæ, 59.
Termitidæ, 111.
Tetramera, 80, 94.
Tettiginæ, 111.
Thecla Butterflies, 63.
Thirteen-spotted Lady-bird, *Hippodamia 13-punctata* 126.

Thousand-legged Worms, 4.
Three-lined Potato Beetle, *Lema trilineata*, 8.
Three-striped Plant-bug, *Leptocoris trivittatus*, 106.
Thripidæ, 107.
Thrips, 9, 46, 107.
Ticks, 2, 3.
Tiger Beetles, 81, 125.
Tineidæ, 74.
Tingis, *Corythuca arcuata*, 108.
Tipulidæ, 77.
Tomato Worm, *Macrosila 5-maculata*, 16.
Tomato Worm Moth, *Macrosila 5-maculata*, 51.
Tortoise Beetles, 7, 99.
Tortricidæ, 73.
Tree Crickets, 5, 7, 110.
Triangular Water Beetle, *Hydrophilus triangularis*, 84.
Trimera, 81, 99.
Trim Lady-bird, *Cycloneda sanguinea*, 127.
Trogidæ, 87.
Trogosita Beetles, 85.
Trogositidæ, 85.
True Bugs, 5, 8, 28, 30, 100, 105.
Tumble Bugs, 87.
Turnus Butterfly, *Papilio turnus*, 11, 61.
Tussock Moth, *Orygia leucostigma*, 11.
Twelve-spotted Diabrotica, *Diabrotica 12-punctate*, 80, 99.
Twice-stabbed Lady-bird, *Chilocorus, bivulnerus*, 127.

Two-winged Flies, 14, 16, 17, 20, 28, 30.
Uhleria, 115, 120.
Uroceridæ, 59.
Vertebrata, 1.
Vespidæ, 56.
Vine-hoppers, 36.
Virginian Tiger Beetle, *Tetracha virginica*, 82, 126.
Walkers, 108, 110.
Walking-sticks, 110.
Wasps, 16, 30, 32, 56, 128.
Water Boatmen, 105.
Water Measurers, 105.
Water Scavenger Beetles, 83.
Water Scorpion, 105.
Weevils, 8.
Wheat Midge, *Diplosis tritici*, 47, 76.
Whirligig Beetles, 83.
White Ants, 42, 111.
White Butterflies, 61.
White Grub, *Phyllophaga fusca*, 87.
White-lined Sphinx, *Deilephila lineata*, 65.
White Miller, *Spilosoma virginica*, 70.
Wire-worms, 10, 91.
Wood-nymphs, 66.
Wood Wasps, 56.
Woolly Aphis, *Schizoneura lanigera*, 31, 101.
Yellow Butterflies, 50, 61.
Yellow Canker-worm Moth, *Hibernia tiliaria*, 42.
Yellow Mite, 4.
Zygænidæ, 66.

www.ingramcontent.com/pod-product-compliance
Lightning Source LLC
Chambersburg PA
CBHW030256170426
43202CB00009B/769